Growing Up Movies....

By
#Clintington

Growing Up Movies....

#Clintington

Copyright © 2016 by #Clintington (Clint Harrington). All rights reserved. Reproduction in whole or part of this publication without express written consent is strictly prohibited.

Visit:

clintington.com

For every member of my family that I have ever watched a movie with. We have introduced and shared many movies with each other over the years and I wouldn't have had the stories you'll find in here without them.

Author's Note...

This book was compiled from a blog. I have not taken the necessary editing care and steps that I would for a novel or other work. You may run along some grammatical errors or jumbled sentences that flowed from my mind to my finger tips as I was excited while developing material about my first passion...movies. You'll experience a similar sense of what it is like to read my blog and I apologize if those errors distract from the regular reading flow. One major difference in the book compared to the blog is that I have had to remove the pictures that I posted on these stories. The pictures that I chose for my blog do not turn out so well in print. Apologies...and thank you.

An Introduction

When I think about movies in general, I think about the VHS, the VCR (no beta), and the rows and rows of copied tapes that my parents and I created when I was in elementary school. We purchased a VCR in 1986. Every Labor Day weekend we would go purchase a rather large amount of blank VHS tapes, rent another VCR and about 20-30 movies for under a dollar each. Marathon is not a fitting term for what we did. I loved it.

The kids were in charge of the *G/PG* films during the day. My mom and dad would take care of *R* at night after my siblings and I went to bed. We would fit three, two-hour movies on each tape (not understanding that this would make those VHS wear out way faster--and the picture was not as crisp).

My dad would always take care of the "setup" (hooking up a VCR to another VCR that is attached to a television is tedious). We made ourselves scarce for that. For the *watching*, we were present. I was also allowed to load the movies and cue them up. It was always fun hitting play/record. We had a VCR with buttons that would light up red for whichever action was in use. The only time two red lights occurred was when you were recording (Play/Rec).

Now that I think about it, whenever we hit pause there'd be two red lights on...when we were editing commercials out on live shows there were three red lights...hm...

* * *

Any ways...I always enjoyed looking at "Play/Rec." It seemed like we were accomplishing something...

I love movies.

So much so that I feel the stories I write about are envisioned as films in my head first; naturally.

My intent is to write and share my experience with specific movies starting as early as I can remember. I am not planning on reviewing films. I'm not a critic. I'm going to convey how those movies made me feel growing up and sharing the chronology (somewhat) of my movie viewing experience.

I hope it will be enjoyable.

Growing Up Movies....

By
#Clintington

"C'mon, Baggy, get with the beat."

"The Jungle Book" was the first movie I went to...and I *do not* remember seeing it. That experience is only remembered by my mother as I was 4 years old at the time.

"Why are you writing about this?"

Technically, this is my first experience at the theater with film. My mother's verbal history on it is all I have to go on; and I did eventually see "The Jungle Book" later at a point in which I could recollect the story and images which will be used to make this a little better (don't hold your breath).

According to my mother:

My mom and I went with a friend from our local church who brought their two children that were my age. My mother's big recollection is that her little angel (me) watched the entire film from beginning to end credits, while the other "children" (sometimes she refers to them as "monsters") would not sit and watch it and ran up and down the aisles, asking for pop corn, soda, the bathroom, etc.

Now, whether I was a perfect child or not, I feel that the engagement of the film itself had to do with my ability to sit and watch it.

After hearing this story a number of times throughout my life, I always wanted to see "The Jungle Book" again because I was curious about those images I could not remember that would keep me so focused. Years later when I was in elementary school and the VCR was invented, I was able to view it.

It delivered.

I have talked to a number of people that have viewed the movie and watched it when they were younger and we all agree on the best scenes: "Bear Necessities" and "I Want to be Like You"

I prefer the latter. King Louie made me laugh, hard. Not only was he funny, I think he had the best song/montage in the film. So, he's funny and I enjoyed the song.

Hearing what my mother said about how I reacted, I want to believe that I couldn't look away from "I Want to be Like You" even if I wanted to. This is the power that film can have on someone and I enjoy the escape that it provides. I started at a young age, and to this day, have not gotten enough.

I do remember seeing the next film you'll read about in the theater at a very young age, and one that will ALWAYS have a special place in my heart...

"How do you explain school to higher intelligence?"

"My 'Wizard of Oz'."

That is what I tell Baby Boomers when I talk about "E.T."

I don't think it is possible to duplicate that experience. There was nothing like it (I know--movies peaked at 5 years old for me--what?!).

I remember I went with my mom and my best friend at the time, and we all were sobbing like two-year-olds after a tantrum when we were walking out of the theater. I can still feel my warm, caked skin where my tears were drying on my face. I know I'm not painting a very appealing picture here, but the film utterly touched me.

So that was the crying. The range of emotions that I went through when I watched the film is what I remember most about it. "E.T." starts out with many suspenseful moments like they are preparing us for a horror film. The mother ship landing, the chase in the woods, the baseball in the shed, and the first time we see *E.T.* face-to-face.

Then the film becomes a "buddy movie/coming of age story" that is one of the best ever captured on film.

Fear, joy, sorrow, despair, loss...just to name a few emotions that drip from the screen.

* * *

I didn't get to see "E.T." again for a very long time. There was the occasional television premiere, but my bedtime never allowed for a finish living in the Mountain Time Zone. The film premiered in 1982, we didn't get a VCR until 1986 and Amblin Entertainment didn't release "E.T." on VHS until 1988. That doesn't seem like a long time now, but when I was a child in the 80s, six years was a long time to wait to see your favorite movie again in it's entirety.

I had moved on at that point to other films that did not wait so long to be released on VHS.

I'm excited to talk about those movies...but in a different way. I feel that "E.T." has set up my interest for every next film for the rest of my life, and for that, I am grateful.

"There is...another...Sky...walker."

I have an uncle that would rather be caught dead, than noticed paying for a movie...

That's who took me to see my first "Star Wars Saga" film on the big screen.

Even my uncle likes the "Star Wars" movies.

When I was little, my best friends were my cousins who lived about 20 minutes away from us in Firth, ID. I used to go over to their house out in the country to spend the night and play G.I. Joes. I know that it was at the end of May after school was out as my uncle had come home from work and we were there all day playing together. That alone was fun for me, then my uncle gave us the biggest surprise ever...but he was a practical joker so he didn't just come out and tell us what the plan was.

"Get your shoes on. We're leaving."

"Where are we going," my cousin asked.

"You'll see. Make sure you have your shoes on, we're heading out."

Now you never knew with my uncle. Sometimes this meant ice cream at the park. Sometimes it meant we needed to go move pipe, dig holes, pull weeds, etc. He liked to keep us lively and ready for anything. It was annoying at the time, now I appreciate it.

So, we got into the car. One of the quietest car rides the four of us have ever been on. Once we pulled into town, he couldn't hold it in anymore and he said, "We're going to the new Star Wars movie."

We all yelled, "Yes!"

I couldn't believe it. I got to play with my cousins all day (which I loved) and then I got to go see Luke Skywalker deflect bullets with a light saber after he was jettison from his speeder. It was better than unwrapping a present.

I was too young to see the original on the big screen, but I was able to see it in bits-and-pieces through it's release on television. We went to the drive-in to see "Empire" (which later became my favorite of the three--there are not enough Han Solo and Princess Organa scenes in that movie; #thebest). I remember being spoiled by "our-cousin-we-didn't-like" about Darth Vader being Luke's pops, so that kind of ruined the experience (that and the drive-in speakers weren't very good back then and the Scout that we were all laying in became uncomfortable in 15 minutes).

I remember being captivated and getting all of my questions answered throughout the viewing: "What happened to Han Solo?" "Where's Chewy?" "Did Luke go back and see Yoda?" "How are they going to kill Darth Vader?" "THEY'RE MAKING THE DEATHSTAR AGAIN?!" "WTF?"

There is really only one thing to say--Speeders are AWESOME and I want one.

I feel that "Return" delivered to its audience on a lot of levels. Light saber fights early and often, monsters crushed by doors, the resolution of the father-son dilemma, Han and Leia gonna get married, The Deathstar got destroyed a-bigger-and-better second time and yes, Lando lived!

It was a year after "E. T." and I already had my second largest big screen impact.

More to come…imagine that.

"Four FEET above her covers!"

There are so many movies after "Return of the Jedi" that I want to write about.

The Dilemmas:

1. Do I stick with chronological order?
2. Do I do a rental or a cinema experience?

I went with the movie I wanted to preach about since I started this.

First off, I have NEVER seen this film on the big screen--I was too young and my parents wanted to supervise me when I watched it for the first time--so I went with the rental. This is not the next film chronologically in my film viewing life either. I have seen this film more than any other film (36 times...I ruined the VHS recording that we copied). I think that I could quote the film from beginning dialogue to the end of the movie. To this day when I flip through channels and see that it's on, I stop there and watch until the next commercial break. There is yet to be a film that was so funny and so creative using multiple-genres. I feel that it is definitely a comedy, but it could have a science fiction, slight-horror tag as well.

* * *

It was directed by the great Ivan Reitman, a comedy film genius and written by none other than Ray Stantz and Egon Spengler (AKA Dan Aykroyd and the late GREAT Harold Ramis).

If you haven't guessed the film yet by the clues in the last paragraph...slightly disappointed but I get it, it was 30 years old last year. I'll throw out a few more hints before I drop the title. It is the film that introduced me to one of my favorite actors of all time....Bill Murray as well as my favorite actress of all time Sigourney Weaver. It had Rick Moranis who was possessed by a prehistoric dog and I was introduced to these phrases:

"Don't cross the streams."

"Are you the Keymaster?"

"I'm the Gatekeeper."

"Ray...when someone asks you if you're a god, you say YES!"

"FOUR FEET ABOVE HER COVERS! She barks! She drools! She claws!"

"Nimble little minx isn't she?"

* * *

"I couldn't help it....it just popped in there."

"He slimed me."

If that last one hasn't given it away, I can't help you...you're lost.

"Who you gonna call?"

"Ghostbusters"

Easily my favorite comedy for all time, if you haven't guessed that yet. I have never laughed so hard at a movie and I remember being excited for each scene to unfold. After I started viewing it over and over, I would get excited about scenes that I knew would be coming up and found myself waiting to laugh for what I had already seen before. I continue to laugh.

Most people remember the famous "slimed me" scene, but I walked away from the film laughing at the subtle things:

"What, somebody blows their nose and you want to keep it?"

and, one of my ALL TIME favorite lines captured on film,

* * *

"Listen....do you smell something?"

The premise and the writing and acting I feel are what make this film a comedic masterpiece. Writing about ghosts is one thing, but to be so bold as to make it a comedy with a science fiction backdrop while breaking barriers with visual effects in 1983 no less (released in 1984). I would've loved to have been in the room when Dan and Harold pitched this script for production.

"Ghostbusters" was it for me. I know that I have already talked about this movie at length, but I want you to know that I have probably spared you a dissertation on the brilliance of every scene of this movie. The subtleties of the comedy they show helps the big laughs be even bigger. I am going to give just one example of this:

Dana, Sigourney Weaver's character, can just walk past her nerdy neighbor Louis Tully's (played by the brilliant comedy actor Rick Moranis) apartment and he will come out and engage with her. Dana's subtle facial expressions show that he annoys her. His expressions show through that he has a crush on her. Later when Louis is having a party and the music is blaring from inside his apartment, Dana tries to quietly sneak past on her tip-toes, thinking that she has a chance not to have to encounter Louis--wrongo. He opens the door as she reaches the exact same point of the last encounter and she shrugs her head down in defeat. This makes their "make out scene" when they encounter each other as the possessed Keymaster and Gatekeeper twice as funny.

To me it is a shame that we don't glorify comedies the same way we glorify drama. I will most likely touch on this frequently as I continue with this blog. "Ghostbusters" is 1984's Best Picture and it wasn't even on the ballot. You'll find that I'm a sucker for creativity, and at that time I remember people saying that they had never seen anything like it. I don't feel that we have since. Definitely one of a kind.

I might just have to watch it again....

"Truck? What truck?"

All right. I will attempt to get back on track as I jumped out of sequence last time. So, to re-cap, this next film was prior to "Ghostbusters" but after "Return of the Jedi." My viewing of this was not on the big screen (looking back now, there are a shitload of movies that I love that I have never seen on the big screen--sad in a way but thank you inventor of the VCR).

As I said...we did not get a VCR at our house until 1986. My aunt and uncle however, got a VCR in early 1985. It was a top feeder/no slide and it had a cable remote attached to it. It wouldn't surprise me if my aunt still has that in her garage somewhere (she doesn't like to let go). I remember breaking that baby in with a film that was released in 1981. It was what I would call a "spectacle movie" i.e. a lot-o-special effects.

The director of these films was always so great at creating mood. From the opening titles, to the music, to the lighting, and editing:

Paramount logo:

FADE *IN:*

* * *

A mountain that matches the logo almost perfectly. A group of men trudge through the jungle slowly as they reach the bank of a river and the back silhouette of a man wearing a fedora steps into frame. He pulls a map from the pocket of his jacket and reads it. A shady fellow behind him pulls a gun and cocks the hammer.

Closeup of the fedora man's ear as he hears his impending doom.

SWOOSH CRACK! goes the fedora man's whip as the betrayer with the gun has it slapped from his hands. Pull in on a dusty--HAN SOLO? Wearing a fedora.

Here started the relationship of Ford and Spielberg that would generate a number of amazing blockbusters together under a new franchise that America was ready for. "Indiana Jones and...."
This particular film was "Raiders of the Lost Ark." I really remember it being a set piece film. Of course at the time, I would just say, "...and remember when they were in the plane and the snake crawled on him," or "remember when he put the staff in the ground and the sun lit the crystal up and showed him where to dig," or "remember when Marion was taken in a basket and he went around the corner and there were 50 baskets!" I think you get the point.

* * *

Looking back now, I think set pieces. The jungle, the campus, the lodge in the snow where he found Marion, Cairo, the sub, the "face melt" island, and then back to the warehouse where all of our secrets are hidden. It feels like a film that had a lot of great atmosphere that needed a little bit of action added to them, mix with a really heroic score from a movie music genius, stir in a french arch enemy and some Nazis, and blow some shit up and we will have a blockbusting cinematic masterpiece that will spawn a new franchise!

You gotta love it.

Of all the set pieces, I think the chase on horseback, climbing onto the truck, hijacking it, getting the truck taken away and having to re-hijack, was by far the one that has stayed with me in my mind over the years. The action itself is awesome, but Spielberg can't just let action be action for action's sake--the subtle bits of humor that he can add to a scene make them classic cinema gold. Indy can get on the truck, cool. Now he has to deal with the platoon of Nazi's behind him in cars and on motorcycles. The little grin that Indy wears when he nudges the motorcycle over is hilarious to me and still makes me grin as I write this. When he is hijacked by a very tenacious Nazi and is thrown through the front window himself, the sound editing of Indy pulling on the hood ornament and holding it for dear life is hilarious and suspenseful--eat your heart out Hitch and Blake Edwards.

A number of other images pop in there too:

The Snake Pit where the Ark is buried.

The exploding plane that Indy and Marion try to escape in.

The shoot out at Marion's Lodge.

and...

The melting Nazis...

But I continue to go back to the truck sequence in my mind after all of those years as my favorite sequence in an amazing action movie.

I remember having a marathon with a friend who had never seen these films a few years back. It wasn't their cup of tea unfortunately, but they did enjoy the truck hijacking. I made sure to ask…

"The TV people."

Between 1980 and 1985 (somewhere in there) we had HBO. One of the big releases that hit HBO was "Poltergeist". My parents, being the protective, viewer-micro-managers that they were, did not want us to be subjected to such scary material and thus have nightmares. When you tell a person they can't have something, they want it most (and cannot stop thinking about getting it until they do; human nature).

Well, I remember the day we finally watched "Poltergeist", my sister and I were both home sick coming off a bout of the flu (I want to say it was day 2 of 3 that we would both be home sick. My mom cleaned homes for some elderly people around town and was out for approximately 2-3 hours on the second day. My sister immediately looked in the guide in the hopes of finding a viewing of "Poltergeist" while mom was out--I think this is a good thing to note: at some point in the 80s HBO caught a lot of slack for playing "adult themed" films during the day and later made it their in-house policy to play those films after 9pm (I like to think that my sister and I had something to do with that regulation). I caught my sister watching that and tried to remind her that mom did not want us to watch that. She simply stated, "Mom's not here." I shrugged it off and started watching. I was distracted as I was keeping an eye out for mom the entire time. Even though I was the "look out" I still had enough time to catch the big scenes that TOTALLY FREAKED ME OUT OF MY GOURD!

There are four big ones in particular that I remember:

1. Dad and mom swimming around in the muddy/bloody swimming pool

2. The man's face "peel off" that turned into hamburger

3. The effing toy clown that ends up jumping on the kids back while maniacal laughter ensues, and

4. The damn tree

Being that I was distracted through a lot of the film and going in-and-out while checking to see if mom came back, I still watched enough of the movie to get disturbed (I think I was 6 at the time). The worst part about these nightmares or difficulties falling asleep at night--I couldn't tell my parents about it. If I ratted, my sister would never trust me again. So I had to endure my fear alone and try and keep it down when I did it because I shared a room with my 2 year old brother. I had a street light right outside my bedroom window that always cast a shadow of our two huge elm trees we had in our front yard. I just stared at those shadows--wide-eyed--until I passed out with total exhaustion. Did I mention the "damn tree" up above? Watch the movie and picture yourself as a 6 year old child of the 80s that has the shadow of two elm trees cast over your windows all night and get back to me. Again, OUT OF MY GOURD!

The film doesn't hold up over time. For those of you reading this thinking that it might be a good movie to rent on Halloween or what not, don't bother. It is more campy now as special effects have gotten WAY BETTER over the years. Watching it again however without any distractions, did help me gain a better understanding of the story, as it was no longer fragmented for me.

I was still scared a little in some scenes--I think that was more PTSD than anything. I'm still glad that I watched it again if nothing but for the nostalgia of it all.

I appreciate that it is extremely challenging to get any kind of "static channels" on the tv with digital signals now.

"Fortune is ally to the brave."

As far as my parents knew, this next movie was my first introduction to monsters and gore.

(Remember, they had no idea my sister and I were having nightmares over "Poltergeist")

I saw it at a friends house at a birthday party. I told my parents afterward, and they were less-than thrilled about me doing so, but there was nothing to be done about it now.

Every time that it was on HBO, I made sure I watched it. My parents were always good sports and watched it with me.

The things I remember most about this film were the shiny metal objects on display as gifts from the gods.

In "Clash of the Titans" Perseus is given a helmet that makes him invisible, a SHINY shield that has a mirror on the inside of it, and a bright sword (it was used to kill bad guys--nothing really special about it other than it was polished and light reflected off of it). He was also given his trusted mechanical owl Bubo (the smartest and most loyal character in the movie) from Zeus and

Hephaestus.

I wanted to be Perseus every day for a year after I watched that movie. My mom took me shopping and I got a plastic toy sword that I convinced myself looked like Perseus'. I started constructing togas out of my blankets, and then I started acting out my favorite action scenes (they were always sword fights, imagine that) in my bedroom with the door closed.

Perseus got to do everything a five year old boy wants to do. Win sword fights, break in a flying horse and ride him to a far off land, kill 8 foot tall scorpions, slew Medusa and the Kraken, and save the damsel (oh Andromeda--I had a crush on you). Remembering these things is so exciting and depressing at once. I yearn for those days again as an older man and know that those days are done, but remembering what I did and how much I enjoyed it always makes me smile. Movies now rarely give me the joy I felt when I watched my first sword and sorcery movie at 5 years old. Part of getting older I guess.

I want to be there with my son with these movies and experience that fun again with him. Will he want to watch this movie? Who knows? I do believe that there is a "Clash of the Titans" for everyone out there, they just need to allow themselves to find it. I'm here to help my son do just that. It might not be a movie. It could be a sport, a craft, music...who knows? I just want to be there to see him find it and help him enjoy it like my parents did.

"...all pilgrims share a deep love of life; especially their own!"

This next one is one of those movies that came out on HBO (when we still had it) and it was an event. My dad and I (as well as my cousins) probably re-watched this on HBO alone, 10 times!

HBO would always (and I still think they do) send out their monthly catalog with the schedule and advertisements for their big movie that would make its debut. By the 3rd week of the month, I had already watched the movies I wanted to see--and had memorized the rest of the schedule. I would yearn for the next catalog to get here, and when it did, it was the only mail I gave a shit about. The catalog would end up housed in my room next to my bed. I would commit it to memory and make note of the movies that I still needed to see and their times.

Yes...I was lonely, thanks for asking...*clears throat*

I remember the ad for this movie and it was larger than any I'd seen HBO put in their catalog. It took up two pages and it had a black background with a wall of fire and the lead characters standing in front of it in the "ready position" with their weapons in hand. This was to be their premiere movie....NEXT MONTH????

Yes, I waited a month. I showed it to my dad and asked him if we could watch it together at the earliest slot available. He said, "Sure."

...a man of few, yet powerful words, my dad.

When we first started watching "The Beastmaster" I was way weirded-out briefly with the opening sequence. A man and his VERY pregnant wife, lay in bed and are accosted by a witch as they sleep. She (the witch) pours a potion on their throats that paralyzes them as she proceeds to cast a spell that transports the child from the womb of the woman to the womb of a cow, in the woods. That's not the worst. The witch takes the baby into the woods and brands the newborns hand with an indecipherable mark, and prepares to sacrifice it.

Luckily, a rather bad ass commoner stumbles upon this scene and murders the witch with a cool ass boomerang type weapon.

We find out later that the people in the sleeping quarters were the king and queen of the land and this was their first born son that will now be raised amongst the common folk of Emur.

* * *

This is a true and total "sword and sorcery" movie that made me want to rent every "sword and sorcery" movie I could get my hands on after I watched it.

None of them were as good as this one. I think there are a few reasons:

1. Outside of a few scenes, there is not much "sorcery" which I feel makes for a better story. Sometimes magic can be a "save all" and that takes away some respect from the viewer and can eliminate suspense.

2. Director Don Coscarelli needs to be given a lot of credit for creating very gritty and well choreographed action/fight scenes. Dar (our hero) is not easily able to dispatch 4 men like they are inanimate. Without help, he would most likely perish in an early fight scene. This is both realistic and suspenseful for the viewer.

3. No forced English accents. Generally in films like this, people expect Shakespeare in the park. Like Rutger Hauer in "Ladyhawke," the actors do a great job enunciating every line and a loss of accent is not distracting, it's natural in this world.

4. The actors that were hired really lost themselves in the material and did a great job delivering dialogue that could've easily made them look foolish.

* * *

I sought out Marc Singer movies after I viewed this. Another film that he did the same year "If You could See What I Hear" is a very underrated story and performance as he plays a blind musician. Who didn't watch the original "V?" And he was huge on "Dallas" as Matt Cantrell.

I crushed major on Tanya Roberts after this movie and enjoyed her in "Sheena," "A View to a Kill," and later on "That 70s Show," where a decade later, she was still a very convincing hot mom. I love her scratchy voice dammit!

John Amos as *Seth* is a very convincing bad ass with a staff and delivers his lines as well as Rip Torn, the villain of the film.

There are masked monsters of sorcery, giant winged creatures that consume their pray in seconds, a hawk, ferrets, a black tiger, and a horde of "Jun" iron masked men clad in leather on horseback that seem like they are from a "Mad Max" movie.

I carry on...

In the end, I was very excited to talk about this movie, obviously. My cousins and I would choose our characters and reenact the battles at the end of the movie with other kids in the neighborhood in our back yard. We had a ditch, so it was perfect.

If I haven't convinced you yet to seek this movie out, fair enough. One last try...

You'll never be able to remove the "eyeball" ring from the depths of your mind after you watch this....

"Right. When you're right, you're right, and you're right."

Writing this essay, I remember what a HUGE impact this movie had on me and my taste as a young child.

It is a moving animated picture full of plot, intrigue, interesting characters, fantasy elements, action, violence, and witty comic relief (thank you <u>Dom</u>).

It is the story of a mother with a dilemma. It is "moving day" when everyone leaves their hovels for the spring as the farmers begin to plow their fields and grow their crops. The problem, her son Timmy has a terrible case of pneumonia, and any attempt on a move from his bed could kill him. What is a mother to do?

Did I mention mom is a mouse?

"The Secret of NIMH" is one of the first full length animated feature films that I remember watching, on HBO, for the first time while sitting in my home without getting up to go do something else. I didn't want to look away. There are things in my life that have stayed with me from that film to this day. There are a lot of cool names to give your pets from this movie. My favorite being Brutus, which I named my first dog ever. He was a pit bull and he was my best friend. I feel that if I ever got a dog again, I'd name it Brutus for a boy or Brisby for a girl. The names are so cool.

Another great name, villainous as it was, is Jenner. Our

villain that shows up late in the game like all of the best of them. I'd probably name a male cat Jenner...or a Pomeranian.

Mrs. Brisby sets out on a quest to save her youngest child Timmy, and seeks guidance from The Great Owl, who informs her of the Rats of NIMH that preside in the rosebush by the farmer's home. They should be able to aid her in moving her home so that Timmy can stay safely in his bed, while placing their home safe from the farmer's reach. Along the way she learns so much about her recently deceased husband Jonathon and why everyone seems to know how important he was...that is, everyone except her.

There are subplots of murder that arise among the politics within the Rats' new society. Mrs. Brisby is caught right in the middle of one of the most important periods of the Rats' community as she seeks their aid in saving her son's life.

I mentioned there was comic relief as well. Jeremy the klutzy crow, voiced by the late great Dom DeLuise steals the show with very limited scenes. He is another line of "lovable loser" that not only trips over everything, he gets used and abused by almost everyone he interacts with.

At the end of the day, the names in this movie stick with you: Nicodemus, Jenner, Brutus, Mr. Ages, Sullivan, Brisby, and who could forget--nay, who hasn't had their very own--Auntie Shrew.

I think the name Brutus resonates with me because of

the affect it had on my parents when they viewed the movie. Brutus, in the picture, has no lines. He is a wild eyed rat that guards the rosebush with a rather large, menacing spear. We see him in one unforgettable scene when he terrorizes Mrs. Brisby when she tries to enter the rosebush for the first time. After the assault, she runs into Mr. Ages who aids her in accessing the rosebush. She makes it clear to him that she cannot go back the way she just came as a rat almost murdered her for doing so last time.

"That's just Brutus," said Mr. Ages as an annoyed afterthought.

My parents laughed at the name, and found it very fitting for the homicidal rat that we had just witnessed. That experience has stuck with me all of these years, and I have always enjoyed that name ever since.

This is a great family film for all ages, with a great theme and story line that maintains a great pace. Take the time to listen to the song through the credits. It states clearly the "key" to unlock any door. John, Paul, George, and Ringo concur.

"...I love you, but we only have fourteen hours to save the Earth!"

I watched this next one on HBO, almost as much as "The Beastmaster."

It was one of my first experiences with science fiction.

Definitely not "the best," but it was still very memorable for me. A big part of it was the bright colors and "enormity" that Mike Hodges decided to use for the sets and costumes.

It's a movie whose theme song was written and performed by Queen, and has a supporting role from the most underrated James Bond ever. Need I say more?

As always, of course I do...

"Flash Gordon" was one of those movies that I watched with my cousins more than five times. Even at four years old I knew it was a corny movie, but we enjoyed it regardless, I think because of the scope of the action. We used to act out the scenes in our back yard with our toy guns...I was the youngest. That meant I had to be Ming the Merciless.

* * *

Pretty easy to kick a four-year-old's ass at pretend fighting "Flash Gordon" style.

I watched "Ted" when it came out and was pleasantly surprised that Seth MacFarlane chose "Flash Gordon" as the movie of John's (Mark Wahlberg) childhood that made the most impact on him and Ted (voiced by MacFarlane). Watching their interaction with the real Sam J. Jones (Flash Gordon) was very amusing. It also refreshed some of the memories that I have of the film.

Outside of Queen and Timothy Dalton, the key scenes I remember are Flash almost getting eaten by a very green plant type monster; the feet of strength where you put your hand in the base of a shrub and hope that a random little critter doesn't poison your arm causing the need for amputation, and of course; the "hawk people."

Looking back on some of the dialogue for a quote, it was hard not to laugh...so I did laugh a little. It doesn't work on just paper, but for some odd reason, as fantastic as the world is, the campy dialogue when presented the way it is, works on this movie...if you're 4 to 8 years old.

I was visiting my parents a while back before my dad passed. We were flipping through the channels on DirecTV and came upon "Flash Gordon" right before Flash and the "hawk people's" assault on Ming. We had to finish the movie and I had a smile on my face like I was 4 years old again.

One of the great memories I hope I never lose being that it was close to one of the last times I would see my father.

Another example of how movies can be so powerful...when you allow them.

"I ain't man enough to be no mother."

Of all the live action movies that I was allowed to watch as a child, this one probably "weirded" me out the most.

I really can't explain why. It wasn't violent. It wasn't creepy. It was an interesting musical, and it was quite humorous.

I don't know why, but it was just weird to me.

I did, still, decide to watch it more than once.

Thinking about back then, there was a lot of the plot that I missed for a couple of reasons. 1) I remember my parents laughing at things that I did not understand to be funny (I was freaking 4...5 at the most). 2) The make up, costumes, and sets were so well done, that I felt I was watching a cartoon come to life (I found out later it was a cartoon first).

Looking back, I'm amazed at how wonderful the then young lead was at portraying a pop culture icon. The leading lady was perfect casting too, as well as the blistering antagonist (who was so good, quite frankly he scared me a little...a lot).

Again, I know I sound like I'm writing about a movie that I kind of don't like. On the contrary, I watched it later and found it much more amusing (I actually got the jokes--however corny they were).

* * *

Now that I think about it, for the "look" of it and the acting..."Popeye" arguably is one of the best cast movies of all time. Can you picture anyone other than *the* Robin Williams as Popeye and the underrated Shelley Duvall as Olive Oyl?

Me either...

I watched this movie before I ever watched a Popeye cartoon...I'm glad I did. It made the cartoon (kind of a snooze) more interesting.

It wasn't the first live action movie I ever saw, but for some reason, visuals from it resonate with me to this day unlike any other movie

Watching Popeye get "rolled" down a hill by Bluto is something I couldn't forget if I wanted to.

Wimpy with his burgers and Poopdeck Pappy tied up in a chair is another.

I remember being entertained and confused at the same time...some of the dialogue is very challenging to understand/hear as Popeye tends to mumble a lot. That is not a slight on Williams, it's a backhanded compliment. After I watched a few Popeye cartoons...I thought he sounded more like Popeye than Popeye...wait, what?

In the end, I feel it is a great family musical/comedy with a lot of laughs and a little bit of horror for small children...Paul L. Smith is quite haunting as Bluto and there is quite a suspenseful scene involving a child and some...tentacles.

I'm glad I got to see it...

...I think.

"There are no happy endings because nothing ends."

Prior to this film, cartoons for me were what we watched when we got home from school, on Saturday mornings or the Disney Channel.

Bugs Bunny, Daffy Duck, Elmer Fudd, G.I. Joe, The Transformers, Mickey Mouse, Donald Duck....

When I watched this film there was something different. It was animated, but it didn't feel like those other "cartoons" to me. I heard a few "damns" and "hells" as I saw my mother flinch and gasp as we watched it together (Uptight).

The story starts off innocently enough with two hunters talking about never being able to kill game in this forest. That must mean there is magic afoot. An enchanted forest?

Our heroine is a horse, but not just any horse (I know it sounds strange, just stick with me). She finds herself listening to the hunters and then has an annoying conversation with a butterfly that everyone watching wishes would just flutter by.....

* * *

The conversation--annoying as it is--sets her off on a quest to find others like her.

See, to this point, she thinks that she is the last...unicorn.

I told you not just any horse.

The things that I remember are the amazing visuals and the dialogue. It is very well written for an animated fantasy tale and as a young kid, I had to watch it quite a few times to catch a lot of what the story was trying to say. I really did have great parents who were patient with me and my questions about what the story was.

Basically, our heroine sets out to find where the rest of the unicorns have all gone. Along the way she meets a magician, a maid, a talking cat (of course), a prince, a king, a wizard, a dead talking skeleton called Skull, and THE RED BULL. Talk about a villain. The Red Bull used to give me nightmares. For those of you that only know red bull as a sweet energy drink, be aware that one of the possible inspirations was anything but sweet.

Along the way there is adventure, action, running, spells, love, lost love, and redemption. I know that sounds pretty simple, but what can you expect from a fantasy yarn?

* * *

I discovered recently that the film does hold up over time as well. I have a six year old nephew that started watching it with my sister and me one night. He was focused as my sister and I talked and reminisced during the film (about the film). He hushed us a couple of times and later, he was quite distraught and full of questions when we had to shut it off early and attend a different event. I felt bad for the little guy. He was so absorbed. I really hope he had an opportunity to see it again, uninterrupted. Or, we could have an uncle-nephew night and watch it together. It's been a while.

One thing I learned...adults can like "cartoons" too if they're the right ones.

"Those were happier times…"

Talk about an animated film that both children and adults enjoyed alike and I will show you the original "Lord of the Rings." It was made in 1978, and in its time, it was a marvel of animation. Ralph Bakshi was the director and he had heard a rumor of the studios trying to create a 100 minute feature of the LOTR trilogy in it's entirety. He went straight to J. R. R. Tokien's daughter and convinced her to give him the rights to complete the animated feature with the proper time allocated that a story of that scope deserves.

I know that this is generally not the kind of stuff you expect to read on my blog, but I do not want there to be any confusion with this version that I am going to talk about and the Peter Jackson Epic Trilogy that was done in 2001, 2002, and 2003 (Talk about the scope it deserved).

This was the film that got me reading.

I remember watching it with my mother. She knew the answers to everything and this surprised me as I had been watching it with her for her first time too and I wanted to know how she had all of the answers. She went into her room and pulled some books from her shelf and showed me the paperback copies of The Lord of the Rings trilogy that she owned. I found that she was such a fan, she read them approximately once a year. They were her favorite literature and when she saw that "The Lord of the Rings" was now available on VHS, she wanted to share that story she loved so much, with us.

The amazing things I remember were the scenes in which the director "painted" over actual actors performing live action and dialogue. He saved a lot of these scenes for the Nazgul and the Orcs that were kidnapping Merry and Pippin. It was both captivating and horrifying at the same time. Cartoons were supposed to be obvious make believe. That is why they are drawings. There was a strange feel to the action of this film when they had the "painted live action" sequences. Adding the feel of live action elements to an animated feature like this increased the suspense and we had a hard time looking away.

I remember being upset that we did not see the story through to the end. This feature raps up at the end of Helm's deep. We miss out on Shelob, the Ents, the Battle at Pelennor Fields, the Gate of Mordor, and the plunge of the ring into Mount Doom. Everyone talks about Frodo taking the ring to Mount Doom, but he never ends up there in this film. We briefly see Treebeard and the film ends shortly after that occurrence.

The film was made in 1978, we watched it in 1986. My mom was convinced that there would have been a sequel by then if Hollywood was going to finish the story.

She was right.

Even though the film's story was unfinished, it still influenced me to find the ending on a different medium. I started reading books and J. R. R. Tolkien's *The*

Hobbit was the one that started me off on that new adventure. I was done completing the entire trilogy by the time I was in junior high and was satisfied that I had watched the ending in my mind. I felt a greater sense of accomplishment doing it that way and decided to make a habit of that too.

Once Stephen King was discovered, I took a break from movies for a while...not a long while, but a while none the less.

The final shot of Gandalf riding down some Orcs at Helm's Deep will be in my mind forever as I had never seen something that brutal before, and in a "cartoon" no less. That's probably why my parents were okay with me watching it.

"SMELL like Gelfling..."

I feel that going to the movies when I was little was a rare treat. Most of the films that I got to see were after their theater release on HBO. This next movie was one that all of my friends were able to see at the theater months before me. I remember seeing trailers for it and asking my friends after they had gone, for specific information....they did not really want to share with me. 1) They didn't want to spoil me. 2) They saw the movie and they were over it. They wanted to play cops and robbers. I was briefly jealous. Two movies in particular come to mind that this happened with. "The Dark Crystal" and "The Neverending Story"

For those of you that read this that are not children of the 80s, you will not understand what a rock star Jim Henson was for us. "Sesame Street," "The Muppet Movie(s)," "The Muppet Show," not to mention "Fraggle Rock," and "The Dark Crystal."

I remember seeing the characters on the trailers being as close to looking, moving, and acting like real life people as I had ever seen since Yoda on "Empire Strikes Back". The sets looked epic, and the dialogue was extremely interesting.

That was just the trailer.

I really wanted to go to the theater but the timing never worked out and we ended up doing something else. I'm sure it was outside and active, which is a good thing. So, months later I was able to see it and the movie delivered. I looked for the strings and could not see any. The movements to the creatures was well attended to in this feature and the story was great.

I really enjoyed the "child likeness" of the heroes and really made a connection with them on an equal level.

To this point, I felt that all things possible in a fantasy type setting had to be animated. Not for Jim Henson. He was always amazing at finding a way to make us believe that all things were possible in live action with the characters he created and manipulated with his hands.

"Sesame Street" to me doesn't seem as epic as a film like this. Don't get me wrong, "Sesame Street" is never-ending and you have to continue to come up with different teaching topics and different ways to teach a lot of the same topics #Respect. I just feel that introducing an entire edition of new characters on a different planet, with a number of different set pieces, on a large scale the way Henson took on this picture made it truly Epic.

As I write about this movie, I feel like my friends did; not wanting to give you too much information about this picture. I really want to encourage people to view this if they have not seen it. If you and your children have not seen it, watch it with them for the first time together. If you don't have children, nieces/nephews? Young cousins? I think that it will be an enjoyable experience. I don't feel that I can "hype it up" too much. It'll deliver.

I hadn't connected with a lead character like this since viewing "E. T." and it was different. Eliott was still a real

child in the real world that had a cool friend that could help him do amazing things. Jen (I know, it's a girl's name, but it is the dude lead character) was a boy who was thrown into a quest and had to figure things out along his adventure and save the only world he knew.
If that kid could do that, why couldn't we?

As we continue this writing adventure together, you'll notice this children hero theme resonating through a lot of the movies that I watched in the 80s. It's going to be fun writing about my theories on how that type of pop culture effects us Gen Xers and how our parents talked to us.

But let's save some of that for another chapter...

"You must learn to govern your passions; they will be your undoing."

I watched a lot of television with my dad in the evenings after I had finished school and he had come home from work. We used to watch "The Dukes of Hazzard," "The A-Team," and "Airwolf." The show we never missed: "Star Trek" (the original series) and then "Star Trek: The Next Generation" once it hit the air in 1987. I learned very early on not to talk until the commercials came on. I used to inundate my dad with queries in between scenes because there was a lot about the story that I was too young to understand. During commercials, he was glad to explain things to me. He had a way with words that kept it simple, without a lot of unnecessary conversation. My dad was not a man that liked to hear himself talk. He was a great storyteller because of that. He had a natural use of metaphor about him and could get his point across, quickly with great visual style.

I cannot forget the first time my dad and I sat and watched "Star Trek II: The Wrath of Khan." There are scenes in this film that can never be "unseen" for me as long as I live.

I have found over the years that Hollywood has done an amazing job with the "even" numbered Star Trek films. No one ever talks about "Star Trek: The Motion Picture." I don't think that I have seen it to this day. EVERYONE talks about "The Wrath of Khan."

The writers got very smart and pulled from the television series to start this tale. Long ago, Kirk left a gang of genetically superior warriors from the 20th century abandoned on a believed to be survivable planet with no technology. We later find that the planet was uninhabitable and almost killed the genetically superior warriors lead by none other than Mr. Roarke from "Fantasy Island."

We get to this path quickly and once Khan enters the scene, the movie takes off from one moment of suspense to the next.

I want to go on record saying that I have and will always love the main cast actors for each and every role on both the series and the feature films. Everyone of them owns their characters and I can't imagine any other actors playing their roles (that's not to say I dislike the new cast at all, those are altogether different films in my opinion, and I enjoy that set too).

This film features intense moments, intriguing monologues throughout from both Kirk and Khan, and my favorite chess match on film between the protagonist(s) and Khan (eat your heart out Moriarty and Holmes).

The two unforgettable scenes that I have eluded to will not be written about here. I would not want to take seeing those for the first time from anyone. I will say this. They are visually stunning, horrifying, heartbreaking, and well wrought.

My dad and I ended up watching this film together many times. It became one of our staples: "Jaws," "Blues Brothers," "Fright Night," others yet to be mentioned....

* * *

I will remember this film for the compelling suspense, action, acting, drama, etc. but I like to remember how much enjoyment my father and I had together bonding over scenes after our first viewing. It was like we were at a concert with our favorite band and they started playing our favorite song right before we saw each of our favorite scenes. Then we would make a small comment on how they made us feel. Remembering those moments with him are truly enjoyable and I hope that I can never forget them. I haven't so far.

"Death and power are close cousins."

This next film has it all.

I thought that "Clash of the Titans" was awesome...I watched "Krull" and it was a smorgasbord of nerdy-geekdom...aka = awesome.

It features a prince and princess whose marriage will be an alliance to save the known world, aliens, a prophet, a shift-changer (they call it a changing), a blind seer, and that's just in the first 20 minutes. There is also a gang of wild bandits that aid the prince on his quest to save his love and world, giant spiders, quicksand, horses that run so fast they start the ground on fire and jump canyons, a cyclops (a BADASS CYCLOPS), and oh did I mention an ancient weapon that will help them destroy THE BEAST? It also features a very young energetic [Liam Neeson](#) in his first role I believe.

I was able to see this feature at the theater and I loved every minute of it. The action never stopped. From the touchdown of the Alien Fortress to the devastation of it's remains, the movie was an action packed sword and sorcery full of amazing set pieces.

Looking at it again, there are a few scenes that no longer hold up. The giant spider I mentioned and the showdown with THE BEAST are two scenes that immediately come to mind. Did they work in 83? Absolutely, but we continue to become jaded the older we get and the better that special effects become.

* * *

Do I still love this movie? Yes. I was captivated by the story, the visuals, and the action at a very young age and a part of me always remembers that first viewing on the big screen every time I re-watch it.

It is very rare to be able to mix science fiction and fantasy elements and sell it as a product (there are no aliens in "The Lord of the Rings"). I feel that this film delivered that and I have yet to see another film duplicate those elements as well as this one did.

My favorite thing about the film is the score by James Horner. Writing about it is going to be difficult to describe, but let me list a few of his other famous scores to give perspective:

"Cocoon"

"Aliens" (which you have heard on every action movie trailer ever cut)

"Willow"

"Field of Dreams"

"Honey I Shrunk the Kids"

"Glory"

"Braveheart"

"Titanic"

* * *

All of those films have some pretty amazing and memorable scores. I would put the score that he composed for "Krull" against the likes of any of those I mentioned. To me it matches the theme, the action, and the emotion seamlessly and it is a big reason why I feel it is so easy to get lost in all of the set pieces that this film has to offer.

Plus, Neeson does horse stunts. How can you look away?

For anyone that is a fan of this genre, I would recommend you give it a shot. Again, if you're a person that lets old special effects ruin a movie, you won't appreciate this film, but if you have the ability to accept things for their creation in film history, you might give this one a try. I watch it at least every other year when I go to visit my mom.

She's a sucker for nostalgia too.

I had to get it somewhere, right?

"Get out of my kitchen!"

Looking back at these movies as I have, I just realized, I watched a lot of damn movies with my cousins.

Here was another.

This was one that we did under the radar if you know what I mean. So I'm just going to say it. My parents were a little over-protective in the watching movies department. They were good parents, but their monitor jive was bagging on my flick focus if you know what I'm saying. Anyways, my aunt and uncle were not that strict (most likely why I watched a shitload of movies with my cousins now that I think about it-duh).

We did attend the theater for this one.

It was a bit slow for me at first. There was a dad that wanted to get his son an amazing present in Chinatown, late at night...nothing weird there. He sees what he wants (we can't, it's behind the magic curtain) the guy that has it doesn't want to sell it so dad leaves. At the last second the salesman's grandson brings out the item he wanted with three sacred warnings (keep him away from bright lights, especially sunlight, it will kill him, never get him wet, and NEVER feed him after midnight).

Dad doesn't really seem like the kind of guy that would pay attention to the little details. Of course, he is very laid back about delivering the details to his son and the last two rules are eventually broken. We finally see the gift, he's a Mogwai named Gizmo, and when he gets wet, 7 more Mogwai pop right off of him--brutal bullies to Gizmo, mind you.

The new Mogwai also start plotting and setup the third rule being broken by destroying the lead character's clock; which makes them generate into cocoons that transform them into "Gremlins".

You would think that the movie would be interesting by this point, but the cocoon stage took way longer (even in the film) than I thought it should. Eventually they hatch and the title for the film finally begins well past 45 minutes into the movie. I have to admit, the gremlins killing the teacher at the school freaked me out. I was 7 at the time and the movie was starting to get "[Poltergeist](#)" scary for me. It seemed like there was nothing anyone could do to these havoc raving monsters that were allowed to roam around the town and destroy machinery, cause traffic accidents, and kill old people.

Enter Mom. (2nd badass to Ripley on "Alien" but I get ahead—you'll find that in a later chapter. Go ahead, skip to it, no one will know.)

I can't remember if Mom killed 2 or 3 G's, but she did it with extreme prejudice. I remember a Gremlin diving head first into a blender full of chocolate. Mom turned on the blender and ground him to oblivion. Then she stabbed another one with a kitchen knife.

Finally, some people kicking some ass, these things weren't invincible. I appreciate the writers going with mom as a badass. I think that my mom would've been too if she knew she had to protect me and my little brother, and that gave me solace. The rest of the movie was just fun.

I remember not being sure whether to laugh or be sad when the little monsters killed old people and caused mischief, and I felt really bad for Gizmo. He just wanted to be loved and he was more responsible than a lot of the people that were tasked with taking care of him. In the end, I think that I was relieved, not sad to see Gizmo go back home to Chinatown.

Those idiots should've never been allowed to look after him. The rules seemed very simple to me at 7.

WTF?

"I don't want to play anymore!"

There was something about Henry Thomas and tears. When he had them, I always had them ("E. T." "The Quest") it didn't matter.

When I was attempting to look up a quote for this movie, I ran across the "Jack Flack's final bow scene" in the list of quotes and started feeling a little tickle in my throat. It took me back and I could picture that entire scene all over again. When Jack tells Davey that he was, "the best playmate I ever had," I lost it every time. I get so damn invested in these things, it's ridiculous. My dad was the same way.

Jack Flack is an imaginary friend that Davey hangs out with in "Cloak & Dagger." Davey is a boy whose mother has died, and he yearns to spend more time with his dad, played by the underrated Dabney Coleman.

My experience with Coleman in movies was always that of the antagonist, or at least characters of questionable integrity ("9 to 5," "Tootsie" "The Muppets Take Manhattan," "War Games,"). He starts out appearing to be heading down that same path as the dad that is always annoyed with his bored son.

* * *

Enter Jack Flack, who looks exactly like Davey's father, only he is dressed in tack gear and wears a black beret (I went and bought a damn beret after this movie and wore it all the time with my camo pants...shoot me in the face).

Davey is consumed by video games and ends up getting involved in real espionage when one of his video game cartridges contains secret government files that are going to be smuggled out of America.

Writing this feels as ridiculous as it sounds to you guys, but for a 7 year old kid like I was, this was a great movie. Again, this is another 80s movie where kids are involved in adult spy missions and being semi-successful, but the family theme undertones are the connections that I made with this film. Even at 7 I knew that Davey wanted to spend more time with his dad. Imaginary friends can look however you want them to, and he chose his father. Touching.

To see Dabney Coleman as Jack Flack supporting young Davey with encouragement throughout the film was enjoyable and made an impression on me with his depth. I thought that he could only play smarmy and egocentric. This gentle supportive performance proved to me and many others that he did have a good guy or two in him.

* * *

Don't get me wrong, I love watching Coleman as a villain too. He is a great actor, and is rarely over-the-top. His villains always have a gentle-venom to them that can be terrifying and seething.
This departure for him and the one in "Short Time" were enjoyable for me. It makes you appreciate what actors can do.

Henry Thomas for me is one of the greatest child actors to grace the screen. "E. T." and this film had a lot to do with that. I always feel good when actors are able to continue with their craft throughout their life. It took Henry Thomas a while, but he persevered and has carved out a decent acting career as an adult.

At the end of the day, I enjoy a film where the thematic undertones come full circle. Davey learning that Jack Flack was and will always be there looking out for him was a pleasure to see.

Even if he wears wings instead of tack gear and a beret.

> "What do you mean? You can hardly see the strings."

This next movie was like "E. T." and "The Goonies" banged and their nerdy kid was reproduced.

It starred a very young Ethan Hawke in one of the most likable roles ever written and an equally young (and slightly chubby) River Phoenix.

The camaraderie that you find amongst the teenagers in "The Goonies" you'll find in this film, but on a friendlier level. There is also the family-fantasy element that is "E. T."

Hawke plays Ben Crandall, one of the most enthusiastic and positive young teenagers that I can recall in a movie. He gets bullied and beat up, but he doesn't dwell on it and allow it to last longer than that moment. "Onto the next *now*" is sort of the attitude of the character and it is inspiring, especially for an 8 year old.

One day he is rescued from the bully by a loner for no apparent reason. Ben eventually tracks down Darren Woods in order to thank him. Darren is resistant at first, but realizes that he did do it for a reason, he's tired of being alone with nothing to do and would like some friendship.

Enter Ben's best friend--the hefty/nerdy--Wolfgang Muller (Phoenix) and we have everything we need for another 80s coming of age adventure in the "Explorers." How can you go wrong with a character named Wolfgang?

Everything changes when the three young men learn that they have shared the exact same dream to the littlest detail. They are given subtle clues in these dreams on how to develop a technology that....you know what, I feel that I have said too much already.

What you need to understand about this film is that I saw a River Phoenix that I was not used to, and he shines. I'm trying to think of an actor with more talent at his age and the closest would have to be a toss up between Henry Thomas and Leonardo DiCaprio.

Phoenix delivered comedy so well and was just as effective with drama too ("Stand By Me"). His comedic timing in moments in this movie is what makes it a watchable film for the first hour of the picture.

The chemistry of the three young actors was great, and all three gentlemen knew their roles.

* * *

Hawke = optimist.

Darren = Gary Cooper--strong silent, effective.

River = believable as a child genius and comic relief; not deliberately, just circumstances.

This is another family film that I cannot wait to share with my son some day. All three of the characters are good people and we cheer for them. They are not motivated by self-indulgence or fame. They are motivated by their dreams (literally in this case) and love the idea of being able to go see what can be seen.

There are a couple of twists that I found well crafted when all things are said and done and the movie ended up being something way more than I expected.

Plus, the laughs keep coming in unexpected, clever ways.

Adventure, high comedy, and coming of age.

Wasn't that what the 80s were?

"You beginner luck."

Without any explanation, some movies just captivate people.

Some movies touch people for a moment in time.

Some movies touch people and continue to move them for years after they are made.

This film touched people for a moment in time. I don't feel that it is timeless, except for those people that enjoyed it on its first release. It is very campy now and does not hold up.

It used to be my favorite movie when I was 7 years old.

It is the boy that stands up to the bullies that beat him which gave the movie its appeal. It's obvious that people like the underdog story. They were very popular in the 80s. This movie was no exception.

We follow a boy and his mother on the tail end of their trek to California from New Jersey. Mom is very excited. Daniel is anxious.

Daniel attempts to make friends, but only finds people

that want to hurt and bully him. There are plenty of moments when he doesn't do himself any favors.

At the end of the day, it is his elderly Japanese neighbor that comes to his rescue and fends off the bullies that are brutally beating him to injury.

In "The Karate Kid," Mr. Miyagi becomes a very necessary friend and father figure for Daniel, and he helps him deal with his bullies, but he also helps him learn how to live his life.

It is the subtle and warm performance by Pat Morita that makes this movie a success. As a viewer, we see what he is doing with Daniel the entire time, but we get the pleasure of watching Daniel discover the lessons along the way from a very patient friend who has been looking out for him since he moved in next door.

You know a movie is a big deal when people quote it.

"Wax on, wax off."

"Look eye. Always look eye."

"Finish him!"

"Daniel-san"

* * *

"Sweep the leg,"

and everyone's favorite, "Banzai!"

I was drawn in by the karate, but there is not much of that. The majority of the film is the growth that we see in Daniel. He is truly a character that starts out impulsive and dangerous, and then learns how to control himself and focus--not just at a karate tournament, but with his friend and mother as well.

I remember practicing the wax on and wax off on my dad's car. I also remember asking my dad to try and punch me so I could "block it." Didn't work out quite the way it did in the movie for Daniel.
At recess in the school yard we used to do the "crane technique" on each other, and I think everyone was Daniel-san for Halloween that year. The really cool kids wore the Cobra Kai Gi (I was jealous).

The movie would spawn 3 sequels that did decent at the box office.

Like most sequels, I never enjoyed them as much as I did the original, but I saw them regardless. I was a true fan and for me to leave this movie off of my list for an impact would be disingenuous.

* * *

I watched this movie a lot and it truly entertained me. I never did take karate lessons and I didn't really want to. I was content with the "moves" I learned from this film. I enjoyed the drama, the humor, and the climax.

After all, shouldn't bullies lose in Hollywood? (80s Child Proverb)

"I'm really a nice guy. If I had friends you could ask them."

Hello Tom Hanks.

That is what I think when I remember this movie.

Prior to this, he was the guy that dressed in drag after work, and the guy that tried to karate chop "The Fonz" on "Happy Days."

Did he make better movies than this one?

Absolutely.

Before this film, he was just another actor, believe it or not.

In "Splash" as a child, Allen (Tom Hanks) falls off of a boat into the water and is saved from drowning by a young mermaid.

They later meet as adults.

Allen does not know that she (Madison--played by Daryl Hannah) is the mermaid girl that saved him or that she is still a mermaid.

* * *

Madison the mermaid gets discovered.

He saves her with the help of his hilarious brother (John Candy).

Allen and Madison live happily every after, "Under the Sea!"

I know, it sounds simple...because it is.

I remember it being a very short movie that was able to keep my attention as a child.
It didn't hurt that I got to see Daryl Hannah's bare ass as she walked out of the ocean.
I remember enjoying every scene that John Candy and Eugene Levy had on the screen. Both gentlemen are comedic artists--no one would dispute that. It was interesting to see how well Hanks held up against these two in comedic scenes as well. Hence, "Hello Tom Hanks."

Watching Levy as the foil throughout this picture is entertaining. The things that happen to him--some his fault, some not--are ridiculous, but oddly entertaining. He also gets to redeem himself in the picture, setting up the ending that everybody wants.

* * *

In the end, this is a very entertaining and fast moving watch for someone that wants to pop in a simple and creative romantic comedy.

Plus, Daryl Hannah isn't asked to talk that much, so she isn't half bad.

> "I had my back broke once, and my hip twice. And on my worst day I could beat the hell out of you."

When I was 4 years old, I remember riding along in the truck with my mom and sister as my dad helped my grandpa, my uncle, and my cousin drive cattle from their corral in Blackfoot, ID to their little ranch in the "Wolverine" area of Idaho. That's approximately an hour drive going 50 mph. I remember the trip taking much longer than when we just drove up to the ranch for our camping trips. We had to avoid hitting cattle, and each one of them would need to be accounted for at the end of the trip.

My dad, my grandpa, my uncle, and my cousin were on horseback for the entire trip.

It took all day and that was only 50 miles.

When I think of "The Cowboys" I always think of that drive we had and realize how safe and easy it was in 1981.

How things had changed.

My grandfather loved [John Wayne](#) movies. I have many fond memories watching his films with him. I generally wouldn't sit through their entirety, but I would take a few moments here and there to watch some scenes with him before I was off with my cousin to play on the farm.

* * *

My grandpa could never watch "The Cowboys" with me. There were scenes in that film that were too hard for him to see and he didn't like to revisit them. I watched all of it with my mother when I was 7 and it was an experience to say the least. I believe this was the first Western that I sat down and watched from beginning to end.

The premise is very simple. Wil Andersen (John Wayne) has some cattle to move and no men to help him do it. He has a run in with a man that is willing to offer his services, but it turns out he's a liar and Wil is not the kind of man to suffer liars. The only help he can rustle up are a bunch of "cow-BOYS" as he puts it--at the local school. The "boys" receive a crash course in cattle rearing on Wil's farm briefly before they are off on their first adventure.

The most impactful portion of the film is Wil Andersen's tough love philosophy around how to help these "boys" become men. We know that Wil has had tragedy in his life trying to raise his two boys that died before they should have; and he has never forgiven himself for that. He is a hard man, with a hard job to do and he wants to prepare everyone of them for the tough road to come-- not only on the drive, but to make a lasting impression in their life; long after. One of my favorite scenes in the film involves Wil helping a "boy" get over his stuttering impediment. We go from life or death drama to out-loud laughter in under 30 seconds. John Wayne made a career out of getting the most from small scenes like this; less is always more.

When people write John Wayne off as a terrible actor, I

always ask them who could've played his roles better? Was he Dustin Hoffman? No. But like Harrison Ford as Indiana Jones, wouldn't it seem wrong if someone else played them? I say hell yes. I also tell them to watch "Red River." It might be the greatest Western ever made and it is Wayne's performance alongside Montgomery Clift that drives the drama.

I digress. Back to "The Cowboys."

There are past characters that reappear and change everything. Namely Long Hair, played by the great Bruce Dern. It is a shame that this film did harm to his career for a time. He is haunting in this performance. I always feel that the best screen villains have clear justification for their actions, however diabolical they may seem--they make us believe that it is important to them. Dern makes this look effortless. The score by John Williams helps this feeling of doom ascend when Dern appears throughout the movie.

In the end, this was a powerful film for me on very many personal levels. I grew up with a father like Wil. I know that he loved me dearly, and wanted the best for me, always. When he had to be tough, he did it out of love. You never know that when you are a "boy." It's years later (after you're 21) that you realize that the lessons that we learn in that fashion shape us to be better people and models for our children--which I am learning now. I really wish that I had more time with my father to share this with him. He deserved more praise than I ever gave him.

"Martin Sheen? That's President Kennedy you idiot!"

Couple of big steps for me on this film. It was my first movie out to the theater with friends that weren't my cousins. I also got to see kids swear on screen for the first time (my mom really struggled with that later). It was also a movie that I walked into blind. I had some friends that were REALLY excited to go and couldn't wait to see it. I had no idea what they were talking about, I hadn't seen any of the trailers on television.

Things I learned from this movie:

1) The attic in my house was boring.

2) Figurines are fragile in all the wrong places.

3) "A" sharp and "B" flat are the same note.

4) Adding a pirate ship to a movie makes it awesome...no matter what.

5) Kids can be heroic too.

6) How to truffle shuffle.

* * *

Yeah. "The Goonies". Still love it.

From the opening car chase montage where we meet all of the different child characters, to the elaborate automatic gate opener, to Data and his inventions, to finding the map in the attic that leads to their real adventure, the Fratellies hide out, gentle giant Sloth chained up in the basement, Chunk being tormented by the Fratellies, the "booty traps" (*That's what I said!*), and a pirate ship...you really can't go wrong with all of this stuff. There is no way this movie gets made today. It just sounds ridiculous. One thing I give to the 80s...they didn't say, "No" too much. Take that for what it's worth.

The score of the film was decent, but the song "Good Enough" by Cyndi Lauper puts this movie over the top for me. It's played when they strap Brand to his chair with his own weight band, release all of the air out of the tires of his bike, and set off on their adventure to save the "Goon Docks". Hearing that song just brings a smile to my face.

It is one of those liberating movies that is both excellent and deluded at the same time. The entertainment value is stellar. The message that kids can do anything and save the day is VERY 80s. I remember being told by all of those baby boomers that we (Gen Xers) could do anything if we "put our minds to it." "Goonies" completely screams that message so much so that it glorifies the crazy kid who never stops believing that this adventure is real and that this group of "The Wrong Stuff" will be the saving grace of an entire town. "The Goldbergs" do an excellent parody of this in the episode "Goldbergs Never Say Die".

I don't mean to sound like I do not appreciate the movie. I most certainly do and it will always have a special place in my movie-viewing heart. I have just observed these things about a lot of the 80s movies regarding children heroes looking back.

I guess that the difference here is that the majority of the movies I did see with the children as the heroes were set in a fantasy type world; "The Goonies" is not. It is meant to be a real adventure in our world in which the fate of a town's future lies on the shoulders of a rag-tag group of very dangerous delinquents. Dangerous is the wrong word...naive? Sure. Aren't we all?

"If we're about to die anyway, I'd rather die fighting!"

I feel slightly embarrassed and giddy at the same time when I think about this next one.

It featured a mainly child cast, with a sprinkle of a few adults here and there as fill in characters and voices for animated/puppet characters. The story is told through the mind of a child in modern day (1984) America while he is reading a book that a crotchety old book store owner gave him when he sneaked in while running away from bullies before school.

The names of the characters are what stuck with me all of these years:

Bastian, Atreyu, Artax (the horse), Falkor, and G'mork to name a few.

Basically, he finds a nice quiet place to read this book all day while skipping out on school, as the story in the book becomes the movie within the movie (even more so than anticipated as the movie draws to its climax).

As a child, I loved the story and the characters. The scale at which the creators chose to tell this story was rather brave considering the main character within the movie of the movie has to continually jump from one setting to the next while trying to piece together the puzzle that will save his world and everyone that lives in it. There are a ton of set pieces, each with their own unique look and feel and it worked because I was captivated by all of them.

As an adult looking back I feel that this is another story told in the 80s that fed the egos of Gen Xers like myself. Our baby boomer parents loved to tell us that we could be president some day if we worked hard enough and they kept telling us that because we wanted to believe them oh so much. With this film we have children doing adult things again: going on a quest, solving riddles, surviving near death, killing villains, and this time not just saving a town, ultimately saving an entire WORLD.

Vanity, much?

So why embarrassment with the giddy?

I'm afraid that this film won't stand the test of time. For 1984, it was great, but the puppeteering and the special effects just won't hold up to what we are used to today, even just on television. I will try this movie out with my son when he is a little older (not much) and gauge it from his reactions. I think if children see it early enough, it could still hold for a period of time with them as they won't be jaded. Kids in junior high these days would most likely be bored with this in the first act.
Do I get sucked into the theme that we need to stick with our dreams? Absolutely. So much so, hey, I started a blog in order to continue to keep writing as a major part of my life. I am a sucker for that kind of story and I did like the plot device of tying both worlds together when the climax draws near.

Sometimes we need to remind ourselves for our children's sake of the responsibility we have to continue to pursue that happiness our forefathers were talking about. It's through our dreams that we can achieve this--even if they don't work out the way we want them to. Having the pursuit of the dream on the forefront for them to see is a most important thing.

"The Neverending Story" bleeds that expectation throughout its action.

So, yes. My son will see it.

"Here's to swimm'n' with bow-legged women."

This film is my favorite "horror" film of all time.

I probably saw it when I was too little, but what are you going to do. It was on HBO all of the time in the early 80s.

After "Ghostbusters," this has to be the film I have had the most viewings of. It isn't just I that loves this film. My family loves it and once we had a copy of it, we probably watched it together in the summer time once a month, after dinner when the kids could stay up late and finish movies with mom and dad.

The open "boating accident" in the film was the hardest for me. I remember after viewing it once, whenever we would sit down to watch it again, I would conveniently go do the dishes or find a need to make water. Next to the climactic kill, it is one of the hardest scenes for me to watch presently. The fact that it is a woman screaming in terror in the dark with no hope and the length of time at which it takes for her to finally be annihilated is what sets the horror tones in the movie. The actress was amazing and what a way to open a film. No blood, no murderer, no special effects--plenty of terror.

I say "horror" because a great majority of the film is action packed with a sea voyage on the hunt to save a small island from this very real monster. The first half of the film is horror at it's finest (I am biased). We get slight glimpses of the beast for scale purposes, but we never get a full shot of the scope of the creature until approximately an hour and fifteen minutes in. This builds tension and drama and when we finally do see "it," the pay off is sufficient due to a perfectly delivered line by the lead character to the captain of the *Orca*. I think everybody knows that line or has heard someone reference it.

This film gave me nightmares, and I had to slightly talk my mother into seeing it. She was a huge fan of the film though and she was torn between protecting me from nightmares or allowing me to experience a masterpiece of suspense and horror the way she had.

Mom was not aware of "Poltergeist" yet, so she didn't know I already had years of experience keeping my nightmares to myself. That helped prepare my parents to allow me to keep watching horror movies as they never thought that I was effected by nightmares. Little did they know I was just trained at hiding it. My imagination is too great to escape nightmares. It's a curse, but I can't stop.

My therapist and I are working through it.

The nightmares I remember always made me feel like my blankets were constricting me from escaping the monster under the blankets with me at the foot of my bed as it latched onto my feet with it's "Jaws." Just like when you are under water or treading water. The shark totally has the advantage as it is their world we're encroaching on.

I remember loving the thrills and the little bits of humor

sprinkled throughout the film by Hooper and Quint. Chief ends up being the butt of a lot of jokes as well and Roy Scheider delivered a fine performance as a lead character trying to protect the commerce of his new home.

Spielberg has a way with pacing an action film so that it doesn't feel like we are jumping from set piece to set piece. The writing and the acting have a lot to do with that and I give him credit for allowing his actors and writers to create entertaining dialogue that keeps the audience focused throughout with a clear flow from scene to scene. This is evident in his films that really work.

You cannot talk about this film and NOT mention the score. I know that it has now become a major cliche. I can't think of another score that we hear that makes us know exactly what the setting is and who we are sharing that setting with (you hear it and you know I am under water and I am going to get eaten). Think about prior to 1975 however. No one had heard that score before. I have only lived in a time after that score and cannot imagine a world without that pop culture reference. Immediately that score became the cliche that it is and it's a major contributor to the sense of terror that makes the movie work.

Just like being unable to live in a world without that score, I am thankful that I have watched that film and know what that pop culture reference is all about.

"You've got me? Who's got you?"

I'm a strange person.

Having gone on this "look back" so far, I have found myself tearing up at the strangest things. I don't understand it, I don't know why, and I'll try to make sense of it as we go along, but I'm not sure.

When looking up a quote for this next movie, I started tearing up when I decided to pick this one. By all accounts it shouldn't effect me in that way. In the movie, it is actually a pretty funny moment. The damsel finds herself hanging from a helicopter that has crashed into the side of a skyscraper. Not knowing what to do, she decides that the helicopter will not stay there forever and she will need to attempt to climb out from it back onto the building again before it crashes to the ground. She unbuckles her seat belt (the only thing guaranteeing any kind of safety at this point) and delicately attempts the climb. In the process, the unstable helicopter shifts and she falls back down, now hanging from the very buckle that had her safely latched in just moments ago. Continuing to clench the belt with all the strength left in her hands while panicking and crying for dear life, she releases as her strength fails her, plummeting to her sure death...when it happens.

From out of nowhere, a man (surely he is no *hu*-man) grasps her in his arms and calmly states, "Easy miss, I've got you," as they are heading back up the way she fell. Looking around in utter confusion, Lois Lane states "You--you've got me? Who's got you?" to which Kal-El replies with a smirk and a subtle giggle that the viewer really has to listen for.

Of course that helicopter crashes down now toward them and of course Kal-El grasps it in his free hand and takes Lois and the Chopper back to the top of the landing pad of the skyscraper.

I have some theories on my emotional reaction to remembering these scenes (some of my favorite in the film):

1. Nostalgia is a tricky thing and you never know how quick, slight little memories of viewing a movie for the first time with your family can bring back joyful visions of that experience. I can clearly hear my mother laughing for the first time when we watched that scene together after [Margot Kidder](#) (best Lois Lane ever) delivers that line perfectly. What else would a star reporter want to know in that moment? Remembering that moment and being able to hear my mom is joyful and painful as we won't have that moment with that film for the first time ever again, but I am glad to have had it.

2. At 5 years old when I watched that movie for the first time, I wanted to be Kal-El and I knew deep down that I would NEVER be able to do that. That sounds silly today as I have had plenty of time to get over that simple fact, but when you revisit things again, I find all of those old emotions crawling back to the surface. Silly and strange. I know.

3. Knowing some years ago that not only could I never be Kal-El or Indiana Jones, Han Solo, Peter Venkman,

or even Martin Riggs, I knew that I could be in or make movies about people like them. It is now a career path that I have not taken and it looks like I never will. Missed opportunities and different life choices have made that a possibility for my past as it always makes me wonder if I could've been good at that.

It honestly is a little part of all of these. I'd like to think that number "1" is the larger percentage of the three because that is a good story. All of these things combined can lead to these silly, strange feelings of inadequacy when I feel that crying is the necessary reaction.

At the end of the day, I bought into a man really flying and saving the day when I was 5 years old.
Definitely wouldn't want to have missed believing in that, however fleeting it was.

I watched this movie with a friend years later after I found that she had never seen a "Superman" movie. We had just watched a remake, "Superman Returns." I thought it was terrible (the remake).

My bright idea was to introduce her to the real *Man of Steel*, but that attempt failed. I'm afraid the pacing was not good enough for her and she fell asleep right around the time Superman encounters Lex Luthor for the first time.

For me, it is going to be hard for anyone to be as capable as Christopher Reeve was at playing two personalities (Kal-El and Clark Kent). There is a scene where Clark shows up at Lois's apartment after she has just spent a night around the town/world with his alter-ego. While Lois is grabbing her coat in her room, Reeve displays an amazing visual switch between the two personalities when he is struggling with whether to tell her the truth or keep his identity secret. It is the most underrated acting scene that is never talked about because of its tie-in with a comic book movie. I encourage you to watch it.

PS

For those of you that did not know that "Kal-El" was "Superman" there is nothing to be done for you at this point.

"Mr. Potato Head! Mr. Potato Head! Back doors are not secrets."

The interesting thing about this next movie is that for the longest time after it was released, there were multiple pop culture references that people used all the time.

Two decades removed from the Cold War now, this film has lost its pop culture reference appeal and is now used to date dinosaurs like me when we quote it. It is one of those films that you watch now and think, "Wow, so outdated." A lot of the things that were covered in this film were talked about for the first time.

Using computers for war. Having computers on your desk at home (I know, back in 1983, not everyone had a computer at home on their desk...crazy).

I'm going to list a few pop culture references from this film:

"Wouldn't-you-prefer-a-nice-game-of-chess?" (electronic computer voice)

"To-win-the-game." (electronic computer voice)

Defcon 1, 2, 3, 4, 5 (5=peace, 1=World War III)

The use of the phrase "Launch Codes" which was used in about a million other war movies after this one.

There's a few. The film was very anti-computer and paranoid with that message. Not only have the people we elected put computers in charge of our future, but they don't have a fail safe if the computers were ever compromised. Talk about putting the public in danger. I think this film is one of the subconscious reasons my parents were always afraid to get a desk top. What if it tried to kill us? I kid....slightly.

"War Games" is about a smart "computer savvy" nerd that does not do well in school mainly because he is bored and has figured out how to use his computer to change his grades. Why work when you don't need to? This general boredom that he has leads to trying to impress a girl (not played by Kerri Green--*sad face*) and he learns how to break into the national defense system from his desk top. He simulates a game of "Global Thermonuclear War" that appears on his computer as well as the national defense system's screen, and they do not think it is a "game."

For it's time, this was a very entertaining film. The public did not have the knowledge of computers that they have now and were easily drawn into the possibility of something like this happening. We fear what we do not understand. Basically, I didn't get a computer until I was in college.

I really liked the acting and the writing and again, I bought the child doing adult things and eventually being the one that has to fix the mess he created. He did get a little help from the man who created the system, but it was his smarts in the heat of the moment that saved the day. Another 80s kid that could accomplish anything. These movies were all over our culture. Of course we thought we could actually be POTUS one day. We could save our town, save a different world in a different universe, and even prevent real life Global Thermonuclear war.

POTUS just seems like destiny after that.

"I'm going to sleep on the FAT couch, if I can fit through the door."

It is with a heavy heart that I write this next one.

I had a brilliant plan. One of my favorite childhood actors was recently nominated for an Oscar after a lifetime of putting in time with his craft. He finally got a role deserving of him that would allow him the recognition from his peers that he deserved. I was going to turn this one in with energy after he finally received the award.

Things didn't work out as planned. Michael Keaton did not win the Oscar for best performance by an actor in a leading role.

....but....

Awards for art are bullshit any way. There were probably 10 people this year that could've won that Oscar. Timing is everything.

Michael Keaton in "Mr. Mom" was such a likable character as the dad that lost his job and stays home to take care of the family while his wife goes back to work. We learned how to do mom's old stay-at-home-job with him along the way. How to drop the kids off at school, how to change diapers, what daytime TV to watch, what daytime TV *not* to watch, and who you should never allow into your life as a stay-at-home-dad.

There is also a great scene where he has to go grocery

shopping for the first time with the challenging task of purchasing feminine hygiene products--classic Keaton scene.

I always enjoy scenes where he has to play uneasy or in discomfort of some kind. That is where high comedy is at full view.

The conflict of adjusting to this new life change is a part of the story, but there is also his wife's boss who is a misogynist that has the hots for her. Watching Keaton measure up to her boss when they first encounter each other is priceless.

The movie is actually a very simple, light-hearted comedy that is fun for all ages.

Was "Mr. Mom" the new American Masterpiece? No. Was it a great family comedy? Absolutely, and Michael Keaton was the next new great actor that I wanted to see.

Which I did.

"An explanation is probably long overdue."

This next one helped me...discover things...

Yikes. That sounds stupid. I'll explain.

It was my first exposure to high school kids gone wild i.e. large parties when parents are out of town, underage drinking, drinking games, etc.

I also learned that Alex P. Keaton does not make a good basketball player.

Yep, "Teen Wolf."

Everything about this movie screams 80s: the fashion, the score, the pop songs. Even the story dilemmas.

The worst thing going on in his life until he discovers he's a werewolf is that he's on a pretty bad basketball team. He discovers he likes being a werewolf, then he doesn't....shoot me in the face.
By my standards this is a "classic." For everyone else in the world, it was cute for a year or two and it has now lost its flavor.

As far as learning beyond extracurricular activities, I started developing major crushes on women. This movie definitely helped this along. Enter Lorie Griffin (cue the angel music):

There is a "bra and pantie" scene that I may have

watched way too many times on the VHS tape we had...WAY TOO MANY TIMES....broken tape maybe....

crickets

I said it helped me...discover things....I'm done.

Ultimately, at the age that I watched this movie, there was some cool stuff that I wish could happen to me growing up. It'd be cool to be able to turn into a werewolf and start dunking basketballs. Who doesn't want to go from awkward loser on a basketball team to the most popular guy in school?

When it was made, the movie wasn't too campy...okay, it was, but we were all impressed with the makeup/special effects and gave the movie a pass when it had a cheesy climax/moral.

The effects don't hold up to today's standards, but I don't think they distract from the story, probably because it is very simple.

At the end of the day, it's Michael J. Fox that makes this movie watchable. He's at home as another lovable loser, but he is also charming so when he has to be confident, we buy it (his years on "Family Ties" definitely helped).

It's a very simple quick watch if you don't want to think hard...at all. It's also good to discover how lax we used to be with developing our stories for entertainment.

Consider it a social experiment.

"Because the band does not have fun there!"

I remember being deeply and emotionally moved by this film (I know that's a-lot-o-adverbs. Sometimes you gotta).

There is so much to this movie that the effect it has had on me as a viewer has lasted my lifetime. I do get pulled into movies a little too much maybe, but there will be no changing that.

Foremost, it is about a character that I relate to more than any other story or movie that I have ever heard, read or seen. He is a young sophomore in high school that meets the new girl in town on summer break and is immediately drawn to her (both visually and eventually interpersonally as well). He has the best summer of his life so far, hanging out with her...and then...school starts; things change.

"Lucas" is short, he wears very thick glasses, is the smartest kid in school (probably the town), is a member of the high school band, and is about to learn that you cannot control who you love; and those that do not love you back.

On summer break, Lucas is Maggie's best friend. She is a new girl in a small town and he is her only friend for a couple of reasons: 1) Lucas is a loner and he allows her to participate in his world, which has only room for two that summer. 2) Spending all of your time with a loner does not expose you to more people to meet. That is why when school starts, Maggie is able to branch out and immediately join clubs and meet people that are closer to her "clique."

There was not a greater time for the perfect casting of Kerri Green as Maggie. She was fresh off her role as Andy from "The Goonies." Having watched that and developed a decent crush on her, I crushed major--just like Lucas--when I watched this film. If she could kiss Mikey and his braces, why couldn't she kiss Lucas? If she could kiss a guy like Lucas (she doesn't, I was just hoping), then she could totally kiss me...right?

Anyways....

Great casting.

As school continues, Maggie is exposed to all of the different clubs (cheerleading, football, etc.) and meets Lucas's older brother figure, Cappie (captain of the football team). We learn that Lucas--just because he is a good person--had helped Cappie pass a difficult class a while back. Cappie has returned the favor by watching out for him (with school bullies) and by being a rare social presence in Lucas's life.

After making the cheer team and spending time with Cappie, of course Maggie starts to fall for the handsome jock, much to the chagrin of Lucas (AND ME QUITE FRANKLY!).

I don't think that this film has become a cult classic or has been viewed by many people out of the "Growing Up 80s" era. So I am going to contain myself from giving away more of the story and encourage others to watch it. I will say you will see a very young Charlie Sheen as Cappie and Wynona Ryder makes her first appearance on film, I believe, as well.

Where you will *see* the movie, I do not know. I don't think you can stream it anywhere and rental stores are hard to find these days. I will probably have to buy it to see it again. Worth it to me, probably not you.

The important thing I gathered from this film is that it is not always about winning, but learning from your experiences (the bad ones mostly). They help you grow and hopefully help you make better choices.

I'm still learning.

"Looks like you have created another Frankfurter's monster."

I think I should warn everybody that I did watch this film A LOT as a child of the 80s...but I'm not really a huge fan of it any more. It had its time and its place in my life and I am kind of done with it. I'm not going to hurry and show this one to my son like "E. T." and "The Neverending Story"

But....

....it would be unfair not to have a mention about it since I did watch it WAY too many times than I should've.

Basically, the American military has created weaponized robots in their effort to win the military race with the Soviet Union during the cold war. Well one of them (#5) is electrocuted in the lab during drills and just "wakes up" later and leaves when everyone believes that he is shutdown.

While on the run from the military, he meets up with the girl from War Games" and shenanigans ensue.

Mix in the fact that Number 5 is now being tracked by two factions: the military leaders that want him stopped/"disassembled" at all costs and his creator; played by everybody's favorite 80s actor [Steve Guttenberg](). I joke of course, however, say what you want about him, he got a lot of work in the 80s; some of it very legitimate. ("[Diner]()," "[Police Academy]()," "[Cocoon](())," "[3 Men and a Baby]()")...and that's how you come up with a "Short Circuit."

What I remember as a child is laughing at how the robot talked after he was able to watch television. He had his regular "Johnny 5 is Alive" voice, but once he watched television and learned other "catch phrases," he could make his voice sound like any that he had heard.

This is hands down a child's movie in every sense of the description. I have no real desire to catch up on it again. I know this because it was on at my mom's one time when she had some of my younger cousins over who were watching it for the first time. I sat down beside them and found myself bored with the material. When I was their age, I loved it. I couldn't stop laughing. This is probably the first movie that I have written about where I feel that I don't have a real strong sense of nostalgia for.

Why write about it then?

I really did love this movie at one point. I think it is fair to write about movies that you once loved, but do not have desire for any more. Taste changes and this movie was my first proof of that.

I will admit...should it be on the tv when my son is watching...I'd have him pause to finish it for sure.

"What? Lit?"

Pleasantly unexpected.

That's how I'd describe this next one.

It was a movie that my friends told me about at school. After they talked about some of the story elements, I went home and asked my mom if we could rent it.

We got to the rental store and she read the case like she always did. She had a raised eyebrow as it was written by Stephen King. She checked the rating and had some concerns, but she let us watch it.

There was a certain scene in which the great [James Woods'](#) character is sneaking around his house at night during a thunder and lightning storm. As he goes down into his living room, there is a lightning flash as he sees himself in the mirror--startled--he screams and then realizes it was his reflection as he gathers his emotions.

I don't remember my father laughing harder at a particular scene in a movie. My dad was always very excited when he got to use the VCR. He would rewind scenes that he wanted to see over and over again. I remember him rewinding the first time we got to see the Millennium Falcon jump into hyper space.

He rewound this scene 3 times!

That outburst from my dad set the tone for the rest of the movie, and we enjoyed it.

* * *

"Cat's Eye" is a movie with three stories to tell from a cat's point of view. It is cast very well and we were able to enjoy three short movies in one.

The first story stars James Woods and the great comedian Alan King. Woods hires King to help him kick his smoking habit. King uses questionable tactics to get his clients to quit smoking. Fear of physical harm to you and all the people you love. This creates suspense and puts our point of view (the cat's) in danger as well. Creative story telling.

We follow our cat voyeur to the next story and he is immediately put in peril. As a "fat cat" dirty businessman uses him as sport, gambling on whether the cat will survive crossing the very busy boulevard downtown. The "fat cat" bets on the feline and takes him home when he makes it across. At home we find Robert Hays who is forced by the "fat cat" to climb around the 12" ledge of his 12 story building if he wants to live after committing adultery with the "fat cat's" wife. Disturbing, gripping, and a hint of redemption. What can you expect from Stephen King?

The final story is the one that spurred me to run home and tell my mom to rent this as an 8 year old when my friends told me about it at school. Drew Barrymore (I knew her as the little sister on "E. T." at this point) is a child that is being robbed of her breath at night from a troll that is the size of a rat. Her trusted new kitty is there to protect her, in spite of her parents that do not trust the pesky feline for a number of reasons. Suspense, horror, and a little bit of comedy in this one.

* * *

I hope I never forget the outburst of laughter my father had the first time he saw James Woods startle himself in his own mirror. It made it easier for my mom to relax with the subject matter, giving us an enjoyable little film to watch together.

Can't ask for more than that.

"Too erudite?"

This next one is probably my favorite movie that I forget about all the time. I can easily say that I have never seen anything like it (even its sequel) and it will never be remade or duplicated because it was so unique and perfect. It should always get a mention in my "top ten" when people ask me, but I ALWAYS forget about it. I need to buy it and watch it once a month.

It wouldn't get old for me, I love it so much.

There were times when I would come home from soccer and we'd have some movies that were ready to be viewed. We knew what we were getting when dad rented them--car bombs, gun fights, car bombs, fist fights, car bombs, and death...except for the lead action star.

...

Just double-checking the car bomb references. Yep, got 'em.

When mom rented them it was hit and miss. She wasn't afraid to give any movie a try (unless she knew it had nudity, prior--then it was notta). As an eight-year-old boy, it annoyed me when mom rented the movies because I was like my dad...action, action, and more action (I was 8, I don't know what my dad's excuse was). We were not always guaranteed an action movie when mom was the one renting the movies and there were some movies that I watched with them that I did not have an appreciation for until later when I matured.

So, as you can imagine, when I came home from soccer and saw the title of a movie that i did not recognize, and found out that mom was the one that picked it out, I felt defeated (I think we lost our game that day--might have played into the emotions I was feeling).

I almost pouted in my room rather than give this movie a shot...

I am so glad I decided to watch "The Gods Must be Crazy."

This is another movie in which I wished I could've been there when they tried to pitch the story:

"Okay, we're going to take a tribe of "bushmen" and drop a glass coca cola bottle (they all used to be glass back in the 70s and 80s) in their midst. We will watch this amazing "tool" destroy their tribe from the inside out until they decide that they need to throw it off the end of the earth. While this is happening deep in the Kalahari, there will be a rebel force on the run from the government, terrorizing the countryside in their wake, as we also meet a cute teacher and scientist slowly bumble into love over the course of the movie."

crickets

That paragraph is the "gist" of the movie...IT IS SO MUCH MORE THAN THAT PITIFUL DESCRIPTION I JUST GAVE.

* * *

The "screwball" humor is on par with Hawks' "Bringing up Baby." I have never seen "time lapse" used so well and consistently to tell a story on film. To bring all three story lines together and complete its telling the way Jamie Uys was able to do with a masterful use of character development and storytelling was similar to what I imagine Orson Welles and Herman J. Mankiewicz were doing behind closed doors when they started writing "Citizen Kane." I also had the joy of learning about different cultures along the way.

I learned a very valuable life lesson too...where would any of us be if we didn't start to trust that our mothers *actually* know what they are doing?

Answer:

Not as well off.

"Whoa, this is heavy."

I am almost as giddy as when I posted about "Ghostbusters." I honestly wanted to jump in and do this back-to-back with that, but there was just so much that I needed to finish before we've come to this point...

...and now we're here!

As I have referenced before, we did not get a VCR until 1986. Prior to that, a lot of people did the same as we did. We would occasionally rent a VCR at the local rental shop if there was a movie in particular that the entire family was excited to see. That all changed at the release of this movie. It was the first time I remember seeing a new release, ever, taking up an entire wall of rental space. That happens all the time now, but this was the first. I had many friends that had gone to this film in theaters with their families and I was very excited to see it.

Every copy was already rented and there were no machines available to rent. It was *that* popular.
First things first, we bought a damn VCR--RCA--it converted into a back pack and connected to a large camcorder that dad used to shoot home videos on. I loved that damn thing. I think we had that thing for 15 years before it finally crapped out on us.

So we came back the next week and there were about 5 copies of the movie available.

As much as I heard about it, I didn't really understand

the concept until I sat down to watch it. Then everything became clear by the time it was over and I wanted to watch it again, right away.

First off, the soundtrack is awesome. The intro and "outro" song was so cool, I wanted to buy the soundtrack, but I never got a round to doing that. My cousin had a copy and I made him play it all the time when I visited. Every time I hear *Huey Lewis and the News*, I grin and think about this movie.

The shot of all the clocks and the alarms going off at the same time is so interesting. Each clock on the wall was very unique and to hear that many different variations of the same sound is quite harmonious in a weird way. This is of course occurring after Marty McFly has blown himself across the room with an amp as tall as a basketball hoop at full capacity.

I used to think he was so cool. I used to wear Levis with an orange vest over them because I wanted to emulate Marty's look. Yes, I was a nerd, and no I didn't just wear that on Halloween. I dressed like that. I also had a skateboard (like Marty's) that had "Back to the Future" on it with a picture of the Delorian time machine.

I never did learn how to play the guitar, and I did try to pull the "skateboard grab the car trick" once....once.

It was a bad idea. I should've listened to my dad, he warned me.

The layers that were dealt with in this movie were quite amazing. I think it needs three views to really catch everything that this movie offers. Once for pure enjoyment. Twice to catch some of the inside jokes at the beginning that Marty and his parents share together as a family. A third time for all of the detail that you find in the "look" of each set that the actors work on. I think I watched it 4 times the first time we rented it.

I remember watching the actors portray their roles in the present (1985), in the past (1955), and back to the future (get it?) 1985. What an underrated bit of work that entire cast showed. Crispin Glover in particular as George McFly, Marty's father.

Lea Thompson was also at her best playing Marty's mother and Christopher Lloyd gave a performance as a character too large for one film in Doc Brown.

I'm at the point at which I don't want to give too much more away. For anyone that might read this that has not seen it, I wouldn't want to take away the pure joy you will receive in watching this movie for the first time.

Movies like this and "The Terminator" that deal with time travel, if anything, give us conversations about possibilities. "Well what if Marty did this instead of that? Would he still be born?" Etc.

Who doesn't like having those conversations.

At the end of the day, I loved the idea of time travel and having the ability to fix things when given the opportunity. It makes for great science fiction, and feeling good after a movie that allows you to think a little is never a bad thing.

"Chopper! Sic balls!"

"Goonies," the adult version.

This next film has another set of young boys going on an adventure together--of sorts.

It starts off with "the writer" of this story as he reflects on a news story that he has just read. It is narrated by Richard Dreyfuss (one of my favorite actors--check out his filmography; great resume) while he writes the tale of his youth about being with his friends.

It seems like a very simple premise. Four friends decide to walk the train-tracks out of town in the hopes of finding a supposed dead body of one of their classmates that was struck by a train. Being that the tale is narrated by one of the four boys, we get quite an insight from him regarding his take on his friends in a very short amount of screen time. Basically there's "the clown," "the chub," and "the best friend." It takes more time to get to know the narrator as he doesn't want to show all of his cards right away. We take the journey with them and slowly gain a perspective of what "the writer's" life has been, and how his friends impact his choices.

"Stand by Me" is one of the first movies in which I was exposed to boys using the infamous "f" word ("Lucas" was probably the first time I heard it on film). I felt that it depicted a true outlook on what boys are like when they are comfortable with their friends and away from their parents. You speak how you want to, you show affection by slighting your friends with mild insults, and you tell a few dirty jokes along the way.

My dad had built us a very nice tree-house when we were children. My cousins and I would play all around it during the day, and then sleep in it under the stars at night. Thinking about this movie makes me think of how I engaged with my cousins. It is very similar. You start out having loads of fun together, then you start to pick at each other--usually out of boredom, then you start trying to be funny or hope that someone else starts being funny; and sometimes, shit happens along the way.

The young actors that Rob Reiner was able to direct, are what make this film believable. The somber countenance of the Gordie character ("the writer" as a child) is very subtle by Wil Wheaton. Equally important is the display of support and admiration that Chris--played by River Phoenix--displays for Gordie (and Teddy and Vern for that matter) in order to help all of them survive the trip they take together.

The original title of the novella written by Stephen King is "The Body." I enjoy that title given the circumstances of the story, but the decision to change the title to "Stand by Me," adds a clear thematic element that allows the opening scenes of "the writer's" reflection to come full circle by the movies very stirring climax.

"Skin it."

"What? Oh God, is it Lent again already?"

I used to think that [Matthew Broderick](#) was the best and only actor that ever did movies worth watching. He couldn't miss. To this day, because of his little hot streak in the 80s, I will go to any movie that he is in whether it looks interesting to me or not.

Man crush? Abso-Frakking-Lutely! He got to marry *Carrie Bradshaw* to boot. What man doesn't want to be him.

This next movie was such a departure for him and his persona at the time, I didn't know what to make of it at first, then I just let go and enjoyed it.

The film is set in medieval times and opens with Broderick playing a thief that is in the middle of escaping from a dungeon through the sewers of what is later found out to be Aquila. Being that Philipe Gastone is the first to ever escape, a man hunt ensues. After fleeing from the grasp of the Captain of the guard, Marquet, Philipe is later rescued by Navarre, played by the extremely underrated [Rutger Hauer](#).

This film soon becomes a road movie...erm uh, a medieval road picture that Gastone, Navarre, Navarre's amazing,beautiful horse, and a well trained hawk start out on. Their first night away, Gastone is left alone by Navarre and he meets the most beautiful woman from the 80s (Michelle "Oh my effing GOD" Pfeifer) who apparently has appeared from out of nowhere and has taken over the barn that they are allowed to stay in for the night. If we weren't intrigued by the adventure and the quiet and stern Navarre helping this meaningless thief out, we now have our full attention on the naked lady in the room--did I forget to mention she was naked?

YEAH, SHE'S NAKED!!!

Now, they're very classy with the nudity, which is why my mom let me watch it, but a 9 year old's imagination is crazy awesome. I was totally content.

Not only was this tale an entertaining medieval action/adventure, it developed into an intriguing story with eclectic fantasy elements for which I will not divulge as I would never take these "reveals" from a viewer's first watch.

This film also has a unique score. I watched this film with a few of my friends and they found the music distracting. You decide. I like it. Give it 3 minutes and if you don't think it's catchy, call me crazy.

Regarding Rutger Hauer. He is the only person that does not speak with an English accent throughout the entirety of the film, and I did not find it distracting. He is such a part of his character, and delivers his lines (and he does not have a lot in this picture) so articulately that the lack of accent goes unnoticed.

Has Rutger Hauer made some bad movie choices? Yes. Has he ever not put everything he has as an actor into every role that he portrays? I don't believe so. A film that he is in can be bad, but I am always happy to see him show up on film (damn--maybe I have two man-crushes in this film--see how I just worked that out).

Recently I saw him on a couple of episodes of ABC's "Galavant" and I was disappointed that they didn't use him enough. He is one of the hardest working men in Hollywood. He has been a journeyman character actor for the majority of his life and no one can portray evil the way he can when asked. Because of that persona, he can play a role like this in which he is the strong silent man that is flawed, but can slay 100 villains all for love.....

...and we buy it.

"Honey? Did you do a lot of drugs before we were married?"

This next one is the guiltiest of guilty pleasures. I have seen it way more than any human being should ever have. I don't know why...but I still like this damn cheesy horror/adventure movie.

It starts out simple enough with a family moving into a new apartment downtown. They meet the grumpy neighbor downstairs, the little person down the hall, the grumpy old lady upstairs, and the nice single lady, all very quickly and briefly at first...but we get to know them all better as the story goes on.

In the family we have the wacky-fun dad, the ditsy mom, the cute little "goldie locks" younger sister, and Atreyu.

Innocent enough, yeah?

Of course the little girl has to lose that damn hypnotic ball down the dark laundry room stairway...

* * *

138 | Growing Up Movies...

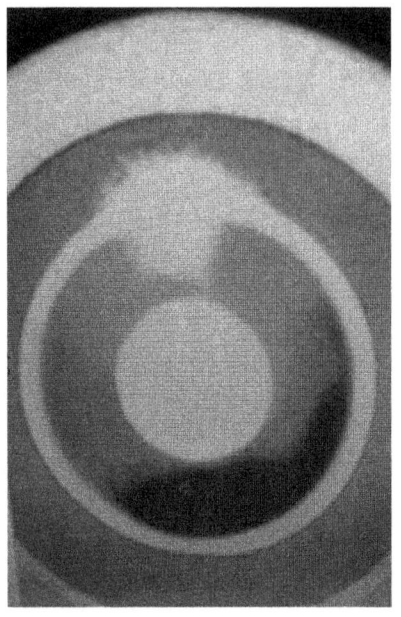

...which leads to her abduction by an apocalypse wielding troll.

"Troll," as ridiculous as it sounds--is much better than the description I just gave it. It's campy, humorous, suspenseful, and...did I mention campy?

My favorite story about this movie comes from a conversation that my mother and her best friend were having over coffee. My mother's best friend's daughter was my best friend...wait what?

Anyways...my best friend and I were playing under feet as my mom and her friend (I called her my adoptive aunt--the best kind) were talking about a strange movie my dad made my mom watch the other day.

* * *

Mom: It had Sonny Bono in it.

MBF: Sonny Bono?

Mom: Yes, he's not in it very long, and he's terrible...

MBF: Oh! ... Is that the one where they turn Sonny Bono into a pickle?

I had to watch this movie after a question like that.

My mother was reluctant...

She let me watch the movie, only after the scene I really wanted to see...she felt it would be too traumatic for me. Mind you, she didn't know at this point that I had already watched "Poltergeist." I kept that a secret for decades.

So mom wouldn't let me watch that one crucial scene. What was I to do? Who could I turn to?

Yeah, no surprise. I watched it with Dad one night. He let me watch the whole thing. The epic Bono "pickle" scene? #Unforgettable

After you watch it once and mom finds out about it, she can be mad, but you get to watch it again...you've already seen it.

This movie had a ton of the fantasy elements that I was already exposed to in other movies. Monsters, magic, forests, elves, prophecies, villains, heroes, damsels, and self sacrifice.

Basically, Torok the Troll kidnaps the daughter of the family to use her as his future bride. He uses magic to take her shape and disguise himself so that he can terrorize everybody in the apartment by turning them and their environments into his magical minions.

Torok is not the only magical being at the complex. Eunice St. Clair, Torok's ex lover is there to stop him and grabs Atreyu as an ally.

Shenanigans ensue, jungles grow, there's a climactic battle, I think you get the picture.

At the end of the day, it's a silly little B-Movie with lame special effects, cool costumes, and a very decent score by Richard Band.

I'm really glad my dad let me watch that scene...the movie didn't make any sense until I saw what sprang from that Bono pickle...wink wink.

"Don't tell me, you got tied up. No. Just handcuffed a little."

I feel like playing Jeopardy with this next movie. I'll list off the cast...then I guess I'll sorta have to be the one to answer in the form of a question...screw that. I'll list off the cast, break it down, and write about it like I always do:

Rick Moranis

Steve Martin

Jim Belushi (Not Jon)

John Candy

Christopher Guest (if you don't know who he is watch, "Best in Show" and "This is Spinal Tap")

Bill Murray

to name a few.

Now, to be fair, the majority of these people are bit, side characters that have one or two scenes, except for Rick Moranis who is the lead. He is mainly supported by [Ellen Greene](#) as Audrey and [Vincent Gardenia](#) as Mushnik.

Moranis plays Seymour as another "lovable loser" that I tend to be drawn to in a lot of films ("Lucas," Philipe Gaston in "Ladyhawke," etc.).

* * *

I need to describe my family in order to give this post the relevance that it deserves. I come from a long line of "blue collar" workers. My father was an electrician. My uncle that took us to "Return of the Jedi" was a carpenter. My dad's dad was an electrician. My dad's brother was an electrician. My brother and cousin are electricians. My other cousin is a painter. I'm a social worker (go figure). My point in bringing this up for this movie is that in general, a lot of these guys that are in this line of work tend to not enjoy musicals. I watched this movie with my dad, my uncle, my cousins, and my brother (my aunt, my mom and my sister were there too) and nobody could look away, nobody could stop laughing, and everybody couldn't stop talking about their favorite line/scenes after it was over.

"Little Shop of Horrors" is that kind of weird, masterpiece musical that never comes to mind when you are talking about the "greatest musicals" of all time (probably because the subject matter is so absurd), but it definitely should be listed among the best ever put on film. I absolutely adore this movie from the casting, to the singing, to the acting, to the puppeteering, to the special effects....underrated.

To have a musical entertain that broad of an audience just in my living room is quite extraordinary. It is one thing to do it with a Space Opera saga, or a comedy like "Ghostbusters." A musical generally is for people that like musicals and I do not think my dad and uncle like musicals (safe bet). They loved this and I heard them quote it or reference it on many occasions after we watched it.

* * *

Steve Martin and Bill Murray do what they always do-- deliver. They share a scene together that *almost* steals the show.

I say *almost* because just about every scene that Seymour shares with Audrey II just about steals the show. Ellen Greene gives a great comedic and musical performance as the damsel in distress/Seymour crush. Her comedic timing with her lines and her deadpan delivery is perfect for the role and Moranis and Greene light up the screen together.

I know that I have avoided talking about the plot. That is intentional as always. I want to encourage people to see this. I hope that the majority of you that will, for the first time, have not been spoiled by the details.

Watching this with no warning is a joy.

"Heil, everybody."

My first war movie.

Of course it was about World War II. That's the only war Hollywood knew how to glamorize.

This was not a film from the 80s, but I watched it when I was 8 or 9 (1985 or 1986), I can't remember. It had a cast of people I had not heard of, but my parents talked about them like I talked about Bill Murray, Dan Aykroyd and Matthew Broderick.

[Gregory Peck](), [David Niven](), and [Anthony Quinn](). I found out quickly why my parents knew and loved them all so much. I learned their names and watched more of their films.

"The Guns of Navarone" prologues with actual World War II footage of the German "guns" blasting ally U-Boats into the bottom of the sea, making a large landing of ally troops impossible in Greece. The footage is narrated by [James Robertson Justice]() with his very sincere and articulate English accent.

After credits, we get the band back together.

This was not the first film to get a rag-tag team of operatives together for a near impossible mission, but it is the first that I saw and I loved it. They were to be led by Franklin with Mallory (Gregory Peck) as his second. An expert mountaineer, he is added to the team to help Franklin and his team take a disguised fishing boat to the cliffs of Greece and climb up over them. We learn little bits and pieces about Franklin's team through conversation and pictures of the men/women as they describe their specialties. David Niven is the sassy explosives specialist, and Anthony Quinn is [Jules' Wallet from "Pulp Ficton](.)"

The team also has a young cold-blooded nazi-killing-machine, his sister, a mute female escaped prisoner, and a man that specializes in murdering with knives.

They run into underground resistance fighters that aid them on their quest (I know you're supposed to call them missions since it is a war movie, but I'm a fantasy nerd. It's going to be called a damn quest!). There is everything that you'll find in your average war picture: a lot of gun fights, espionage, betrayal, capture, escape, and explosions.

This was a good shuffle for me in the types of films I was consuming as a child and the story, the suspense, the acting, and the twists were what kept me focused.

It is quite a lengthy picture at a running time of 158 minutes and the pacing will seam very slow by modern standards.

My advice--if you are interested--is to plan the time to watch it, alone with no distractions, and really listen to the dialogue (especially Niven's lines--he has some great ones). It is very well written and every bit of dialogue is important to the tension of the story. If you need to stop it and take a break, do it and come back to it later.

* * *

At the age that I watched it, it was a great spectacle film for me. I also enjoyed the chemistry the actors shared, along with the subtle relationships that all of the characters had. How this team interacted within itself is part of the allure that drives the action vehicle and creates incredible drama.

Plus, it's cool to watch them blow up some shit.

"...I'll go, I'll go, I'll go, I'll go, I'll go...."

This movie is one for the ages and it stands the test of time. I have talked to many people from different generations Boomers, Gen-Xers (for sure), and even Millennials...all of them love it (not so many Traditionalists--can't please everybody).

This is arguably, along with "Ghostbusters" and "Back to the Future" the best "80s film" of all time. When I say "80s film" I mean when you watch it you see the 80s (hair styles, cars, dress, etc.) and there is a strong sense of nostalgia for the viewer and that specific time period when they remember first seeing that movie.

For me, there was a lot of tension when I first watched it.

My mother was opposed to allowing us to view it. She knew that it was a movie about a kid that made skipping school an extracurricular, and that he made "authority figures" look like morons. I think my sister spent an hour talking my mother into allowing us to watch it. She finally gave in.

At the end of the day, I was like, "What's the big deal? I guess I will *never* see 'Porky's'...."

My first viewing was challenging through all of the judgmental gasps that my mom had to throw at it. At one point, we were able to get it copied and I was able to watch it with no distractions.

* * *

I think I watched it back-to-back.

I remember laughing at so many things and having a hard time thinking of my "favorite part."

Generally I define my "favorite part" as that scene you always want to talk about with your friends as you are walking out of the theater.

"Ferris Bueller's Day Off" was my "favorite part." Even the end credits and the final conversation Ferris has with us after the movie is over-over.

For me, Ferris Bueller was a teenager's James Bond. I remember people describing the Bond character as a, "man that women want, and a man that men want to be." Ferris was the teenager that all the teenage girls wanted, and all of the teenage boys wanted to be him.

He was smarter than every adult in the film (What teenager doesn't dream of making every authority figure they come up against look like a fool?), great things just fell into his lap, and even his sister--WHO HATES HIM--comes around on her opinion of him at the end.

Some of the biggest laughs in the movie come from a very underrated comedic actor in Jeffrey Jones as Ed Rooney. His ability to play a straight-man, buffoon is unrivaled. The scenes at Ferris's home without a lot of interaction with other actors are hilarious displays of slap stick and facial expressions that make the sternest people giggle (my dad).

Add in Alan Ruck in a role of a lifetime as Ferris's

sidekick/heterosexual life partner (for this movie any way) and you have one of the most perfectly cast films of all time.

What I found again was a character I could relate to in Cameron Frye. The boy who was actually sick that was willing to do anything for his friend; including being the third wheel on their adventure to Chicago with Ferris's girlfriend in tow. We all want to be Ferris, most of us are Cameron. Things don't always go right for us the way they do for Ferris, but we know we're lucky to have a friend like him and would be willing to do anything to keep him.

At the end of the day, I don't believe that Ferris's day was selfish. I think he sincerely did this for Cameron knowing the ins-and-outs of his friend's home life. He just wanted to give him a great day and tried the only way a child of privilege knew how.

Trust me, there is an entire other chapter that I could fill about this movie regarding Ferris' sister's journey as well, but I don't want to indulge too many crucial points.

I will say, this movie made Charlie Sheen.

He has what I would consider at the time a "bit part". We look back at it now as a cameo, but Charlie Sheen was not as well known as he is now when he has that very small scene with Ferris's sister. Talk about a well crafted scene. Without even trying, that first closeup of him sitting on that couch next to her just uncomfortably staring at her is priceless.

* * *

For a movie as funny and at times as farcical as it is, to have the heart that it has in the end in Cameron's father's garage is at times a rare choice in Hollywood. It's that choice that made this film the classic that it has become.

"Fix the cigarette lighter."

This next movie was watched much later than its initial release. My parents wanted to wait until my humor was mature enough to understand all of the jokes. After surviving "Ferris Bueller's Day Off," they must've felt I was ready.

The circumstances under which we rented it for my first viewing were rather funny. I remember having a discussion with my dad about [Carrie Fisher](#) (I called her Princess Leia) when we were watching "Star Wars." We were talking about how we never saw her in movies any more. Then my dad said, "She was the woman who couldn't shoot in 'The Blues Brothers.'"

He told me about the scene and we decided that it would be the next movie we'd rent.

Carrie Fisher's character was a very small part of a rather ludicrous, comedic masterpiece.

Everyone that has seen this movie talks about the amazing musical numbers from some of the greatest stars in soul music history. Ray Charles, Aretha Franklin, James Brown, Cab Calloway, and of course, the Blues Brothers.

"Everybody Needs Somebody to Love" is a performance that you can't help smiling at when you're watching it happen. Check out Dan Aykroyd, that guy could really dance back then.

* * *

For me, like my dad--because of him in a way--I will never forget the very brief and hilarious Carrie Fisher moments in the film.

Her character never really gets a proper introduction until way later in the film. This adds to the "ludicrous" element I was talking about as she is just a random woman that is attempting to kill the Blues Brothers for all we can see. The bold way in which she goes about it is what adds to the overall farce of this movie; which is a huge part of its charm.

It is a movie that has everything in it. A load of laughs, amazing music, live performances by legendary artists, dancing, gun fights, car cha--sorry--EPIC car chases, and a cameo by Steven Spielberg as an actor.

It will be a movie that I will never forget, and can always hold dear in my heart. My dad introduced me to this picture and it was the last film that he and I shared as viewers together before his passing. It was an amazing evening of just sitting and enjoying a hilarious movie together while talking about the scenes we couldn't wait for. Even though we had seen it over 10 times, we still laughed.

...and that is everything you want from a comedy.

"Are all American officers so ill mannered?" - "Yeah, about 99 percent."

The next war movie I watched, didn't much feel like one.

It took place in a German POW camp and all of the heroes were prisoners. The one message I think I took from this movie was, German prisons ain't so bad.

It seemed like most of the guards were either stupid or aloof, and the prisoners were free enough to develop such an elaborate plan as creating 3 tunnels (Tom, Dick, and Harry) out, so that all 250 prisoners could escape. There was very much a sort of, "Now shame on you prisoners for trying to escape from my nice little prison. Do you know how that made me feel? I want you to go sit in the cooler and think about how that made me feel." You never saw anyone get beaten or tortured. One prisoner makes a break for it by literally trying to climb the fence in front of everybody giving them no choice but to shoot him, but I had a hard time seeing the motivation for that character to act out like that and felt that it was a manipulation scene by the screenwriter to develop a little bit of urgency in the rather long film.

I don't mean to sound like I didn't enjoy the picture. There were many classic elements created here. Some even inspired Stephen King to write the novella for the "Shawshank Redemption."

As out of place as the score for the picture is, it is totally a catchy tune that I enjoy listening to. I feel that it doesn't really set the proper tone though for a POW camp, where escape could mean death. It sets more of a tone that is "hey, look at all of these silly little allies and their shenanigans."

"The Great Escape" does offer many things, foremost being the cast: Steve McQueen, James Garner, Charles Bronson, and James Coburn for starters. For those of you that are not aware of who these people are, I suggest you check the links and look at their work. Just these four names from the film hold at least a dozen movies worth watching from their resume's combined.

There is a bit of suspense in this picture, as well as some amazing motorcycle stunts, and gun fights.

Looking back I feel that this film was another bit of glorification for the "Greatest Generation," which is not a bad thing, but it did not feel like a real POW camp like "Stalag 17." For a real atmosphere of fear, despair, distrust, and survival, I would suggest that movie.

For a great cast, witty writing, a large scale, and some decent action enjoy "The Great Escape."

"...Presents"

My parents were watching what I felt was a rather ODD movie when I walked into the living room one random evening after dinner.

There was a woman in a daze. Cut to a little girl walking into a room (that she probably was not supposed to walk into). Back to the woman in a daze. Cut to a little girl witnessing "abuse" between a man against a woman. Dazed woman one last time and cut back to a little girl with a blood-stained fire poker with a dead man on the floor.

I may not have all of the details correct. I have never seen this film in it's entirety, other than that brief moment when I was a child almost 29 years ago.

I asked my mother what she was watching and she said, "It's called 'Marnie' and it has Sean Connery in it." Years later I found out that she didn't like that movie, but she wanted to look at Connery....go figure.

Slightly intrigued, I asked her what was going on and she said, "The typical things you'd find in a Hitchcock film... flashbacks, murder, suspense."

I really stopped listening at "Hitchcock." I was curious why she would assume I knew what a "Hitchcock film" was. So I asked her and she mentioned "Alfred Hitchcock Presents" and gave me a short bio in terms of the suspense that he was known for.

* * *

My dad butted in and said, "He did 'The Birds'. We'll rent that this weekend. It's way better than this."

We did.

I remember that once the heroine, played by Tippi Hedren, realized what was going on with the birds, that I was anxious with anticipation for each scene that followed until the end.

I remember being disappointed with the ending, because I felt it did just that...it ended without any "real" resolution. It wasn't until years later when I was watching a special on Hitchcock that someone pointed out that in an era in film when "THE END" was always superimposed on the last few frames of every picture, Hitchcock did not do that in "The Birds." So, given its time period, that makes for a very ominous and overwhelming ending for a horror picture.

Subtle brilliance.

After that experience, I rented at least one Hitchcock picture on every rental outing until we ran out of options at the rental store. In one summer I think I watched 9 Hitchcock films. NOTE: the only one mom would not let me see was "Psycho." (shocking--I know.)

"North By Northwest"

One of my favorites. A man, Cary Grant, is set up to be a patsy for things larger than him in the world and has to figure things out along the way in order to clear his name.

* * *

"The Man Who Knew Too Much"

Not one of the best, but it has its moments. It stars Jimmy Stewart who gets caught up in overhearing minor details in an assassination plot while vacationing with his family. He of course has to get involved and try and prevent the murder.

"Vertigo"

Not my *very* favorite Hitchcock, but it is probably number two on the list. It also stars Jimmy Stewart as a man that is asked to follow a woman to ensure that she does not harm herself with suicide. Stewart becomes obsessed with her as he watches her and if you think I'm going to give anything else away you're crazy. This is widely considered a "Classic Must See" and everyone needs to find it and watch it if you are any kind of movie fan that wants to learn about the art of cinema.

Masterpiece, easily.

—

I was just 8 years old (1985) when Jimmy G. ruined "Psycho" for me.

(*Originally I had the dialogue of the actual spoil that occurred in 1985, but I omitted it because I didn't want to do the same to any of you. Who says I don't care?*)

I was too young to realize I should have been angry, not confused.

* * *

Years later when my parents finally allowed me to see it, I *was* angry. It could've been the scariest movie of all time for me, but instead, it was...*okay, had to delete this too.*

I admit it, I don't like to get spoiled. That's why I'm not a huge fan of trailers much any more. They give too much away (especially in comedies) and it ruins the theatrical experience of "shock and awe."

That is the fuel that fired up Mr. Hitchcock.

How can I shock people into "awe?"

Some of his other films that I watched that summer were:

"Strangers on a Train"

Classic Hitchcock. Two men who each need someone "out" of their lives, meet on a train. The one gentleman (the naive one--there is always one in a Hitch movie), thinks it a mere coincidence, but he has been stalked by the other gentleman. They do what a lot of people do in Hitchcock films, get onto the topic of murder and discuss how to commit one. That's all you're getting. Go see it.

"Frenzy"

I feel this was the master's last great film (this was his second to last film, the last being "Family Plot" which I did not like the acting in particular). There are MANY brutal murders (there is a serial killer who strangles people with his neck ties) and a case of mistaken identity/wrongfully accused. Watch it. It's horrifying.

...and...

My favorite Hitch of all time:

"REAR WINDOW"

I love this movie. It was one of the last ones I had seen that summer. I remember every time that I tried to rent it, it was not available. It was finally in the store and I felt like it was Christmas. We rented 7 Hitchcock films before I could watch it! After seeing it, I knew why it was always gone. In terms of setting, it is Hitch's greatest achievement. An adventurous photographer is home-bound at his apartment loft in a wheelchair after he broke is leg on the job. His only contact is with his girlfriend, played by *the* Princess Grace Kelly, and his maid. He entertains himself by breaking out one of his large telephoto lenses and "peeps" on his neighbors across the way at another complex. It's a Hitchcock movie. What could he possibly see? There is no way I am writing another word about it.

MUST SEE.

It was one of the best summers of movie rentals I ever experienced. My mom, dad, and I would talk about them right after we finished and would ask each other things like, "Why did he do that," "Who writes these things," "Remember when ... happened," and "What was she thinking?"
These weren't the only Hitch films I watched. I would

eventually see "Shadow of a Doubt," "Rope," and "Notorious." I recommend all three, especially "Notorious." Cary Grant plays a very different character than what you are likely used to seeing on screen--as only Hitch could force him to do; and Ingrid Bergman shines as a spy, forced into a very dangerous circumstance.

Hitch's movies will appear to "drag" by today's standards. They are full of a lot of "explaining" dialogue that distracts from the flow of the story, even in Hitch's time of film making (the last explanation in "Psycho" by the doctor explaining the psychology of it all absolutely destroyed a near perfect film).

With that said, the scenes where Hitchcock ensnares us as the viewer and dares us to look away make all of the "explaining" and the lengthy monologues well worth the wait for the "*AWE*" moments.

"YOU WERE A TOMATO!"

THIS MOVIE...sorry left the caps lock on from the quote.

This movie made me think about trying an acting career (that was short lived) but I thought about it. To see Dustin Hoffman transform himself in such a way was a sensation. Casting against type is one thing, and like Alec Guinness before him, Hoffman proved there is no "type" for actors like them.

In "Tootsie," Michael Dorsey is a struggling "method" actor that is having a hard time finding anyone willing to work with him, due to his need for "motivation" behind every character that he will have to portray. He cannot get work in New York or Los Angeles and word has gotten around that he is impossible to work with, so much so that even parts for extras on stage are not available for the very talented artist.

After having a very real conversation with his agent, played by the amazing director Sydney Pollack, Michael realizes he has to change things; and man does he.

He finds that there are open casting calls for a soap opera that is filming locally and he goes, auditions, and gets cast. First, he puts on his makeup, his wig, his high heels, and his skirt, and gets cast as Emily Kimberly, his/her stage name now is Dorothy Michaels. So we have a very Shakespearianesque set of layers here. Michael is a man, dressed as a woman (Dorothy Michaels), playing the part of Emily Kimberly on the soap opera *Southwest General*; the play within the play if you will.

Imagine the shenanigans that might ensue.

This movie had a lot of people that were fairly young in their careers and it made them stars. To name a few: Teri Garr, Jessica Lange, Geena Davis, and Bill Murray (Murray already had a "career" having done *SNL*, "Meatballs," "Caddyshack," and "Stripes," but he hadn't done "Ghostbusters" yet so....). We also see Dabney Coleman again as the sexist director of the soap.

Given his limited time on screen, Murray still manages to get one of the best lines in the movie, and Jessica Lange shines as the actress on set that Michael falls for while playing Dorothy Michaels playing Emily Kimberly on *Southwest General*.

I learned what situational comedy was when I watched this. Living the life that Michael does as soon as he commits, not only changes his career, but how he will view the world. Watching characters grow like that on screen is great, and getting to learn something along the way with them is always fun.

I think I love slapstick comedy because of this movie--and Abbott and Costello of course.

Given the set of circumstances that Michael finds himself in now leads the way for misunderstandings, revelations, outcries, and hearts to be broken.

Shakespeare, eat your heart out.

"Someone's gonna get killed, and you're farting around with prehistoric animals."

I always called this next one, "Raiders Lite."

The opening montage of the film is hilarious. It is narrated by our lead character (unbeknownst to us in a first viewing). The scene unfolds and a very vile man is going to rape and murder a faceless woman, until she pulls out a hidden knife from her boot, lets it fly and kills him in a single blow. She eventually ends up in the arms of her tall, dark, stranger lover...the end.

What?

Cut to a "homely" looking Kathleen Turner, crying away at her typewriter. She is Joan Wilder, novelist. She has just completed another one of her Romance Novels.

She receives a strange manila envelope in the mail that she disregards at first, until she receives a call from her distraught sister who lets her know that if she does not bring the contents of the envelope (a treasure map) to Columbia, the men keeping her will kill her.

The many things I remember about "Romancing the Stone" are this:

In the 80s, try to make Kathleen Turner look "homely" at all; she's still more beautiful than most women on their best "made up" day.

* * *

Danny DeVito is hilarious, and this was my introduction.

Michael Douglas does a pretty good Indiana Jones impression.

My mom would continue to fastforward through any sex scene, nudity or not.

"Look at those snappers!"

This movie is a smorgasbord of everything Hollywood expects from their blockbusters: beautiful leads, high adventure, subtle moments of brilliant comedic timing (mainly by DeVito), well written dialogue (even the cheesy Romance Novel stuff; it is a wink to us from the writers given the lead character's profession), larger than life set pieces (the mud slide, the car floating on the river, the Colombian landscapes), and action.

Joan, out of the gate, is not built for these adventures. Can she write them? Hell yes. Can she star in one of her books? No. She wore heels to the jungle. In a rare set of circumstances that only happens in romance novels or Hollywood, Joan runs into Jack "Trustworthy" Colton. The two are stranded in the jungle, and he agrees to help her get to a phone.

Based on the title, you know what's going to happen. When two beautiful people meet in the jungle in the middle of a Hollywood movie...come on. Romance baby!

The performances by Douglas, Turner, and DeVito are

what keep the story moving.

Turner's *Joan* is a very delicate creature that only wants to save her sister, and realizes early that she can't do it alone. Douglas's *Colton* is a cryptic vagabond that wants to do the right thing...or does he? Hence, "cryptic." DeVito's *Ralph* is a man put in a situation he'd rather not be in (he is part of the gang that has kidnapped Joan's sister and has to ensure that she gets the map to them safely). *Ralph* of course gets mixed up with the dirty Columbian cop that has tracked Joan from her apartment in America and back to Columbia again. In the midst of all of that, *Ralph* is used and abused for our comedic benefit--and we appreciate his labors. The faces that DeVito can make would seem "over-the-top" or "too big" if made by any other actor. We buy it every time he widens those dark brown eyes in rage or panic. Priceless.

In the end, this movie is full of shenanigans from one scene to the next. Do we buy all of them? Not really, but we sure as hell want to if not simply for the high entertainment we are put through from start to finish.

Remember, "Look at those snappers!"

Advice to live by...right Zolo?

"Do not speak to me of rules."

This was my first taste of a "real" war movie.

Hollywood was very good at glamorizing the allies World War II efforts. "We" win, the villainous Japanese/Germans die. The allies were heroic, the enemy was often faceless or sniveling when they got screen time. Allies rarely died and when they did, it was a sacrifice to save many.

This picture was not like that.

On my film history soap box. Bare with me.

David Lean was a master of "The Epic Film." Cecil B. Demille was credited with being that, but to me, he set the stage for the real master to take over that title. Lean's epics were grand and had amazing stories to tell. Demille got caught up in the spectacle of it all and his scenes always felt like reasons to justify "bigger" and "bigger." Lean used a large scale, but he always centered it around a great story.

Demille directed:

"The Ten Commandments," and "The Greatest Show on Earth," two indisputable "epics." The rest of his pictures are debatable regarding that definition.

Lean directed:

"Great Expectations," "Oliver Twist," "Summertime,"

"[Lawrence of Arabia]()," "[The Greatest Story Ever Told](),"
"[Doctor Zhivago]()," and "[A Passage to India]()."

Of this list, "Summertime" does not appear to sound like an "Epic," but once you have seen the cinematography choices that Lean made, you realize that it is.

Off my soap box, back to the picture.

"The Bridge on the River Kwai" is the other Lean epic that I did not add to the list above. The setting is another POW camp full of British Officers that are tasked under forceful labor to construct a new bridge to aid the Japanese in a supply effort. This POW camp setting feels like a POW camp. People are tortured, beaten, disrespected, embarrassed, harassed, and killed.

Instead of a "cooler" like in the "[Great Escape]()," they use an "oven," a small insulated encased box that does not give you room to lay down in sitting out in the open of the hot sun. You can smell the torture of it the first time they take Colonel Nichols (played by the great Alec Guinness) out of it from a short stay.

[Alec Guinness]() to me was just Obi-Wan Kenobi prior to this film. I was talking to my grandma about how I didn't like old actors as much as the newer ones. They just "seem realer" to me and she said, "Oh, really, what about Sir Alec Guinness?"

I said, "Who's that?"

"I don't know if you've seen anything he was in," she said.

* * *

My mom piped in and said, "He's Ben Kenobi from Star Wars."

I said, "Oh...what should I watch?"

Without hesitation my grandmother said, "'The Bridge on the River Kwai,' you watch that and tell me whether or not you like 'old' actors."

Dammit she was right. I became obsessed with Alec Guinness and tried renting as many of his movies that I could find. I look back at the original "Star Wars" and realized the expression choices that he made just under the surface. When you view a space opera, you don't necessarily remember the acting, you look at the spectacle of it all and reminisce about those scenes. After seeing him in "Bridge," I started watching all of his movies with an intent focus on him and his approach. I think he's my favorite actor.

Not only did this film open my eye to Guinness and his filmography, it changed the way I felt about war movies. I left with a very eerie, uneasy feeling, and I think that was-no, *is*-a good thing.

The closing line of the film exudes what we should always ponder before we make the decision to go to war.

"I never joke about my work, 007."

I mean, we have to talk about James Bond, right?

Much like we handled Hitchcock, we did the same with James Bond. I remember my mom watching "Dr. No" one night and I asked her about it. She said, "This is the first James Bond movie."

What is this *James Bond* you speak of?

I sat and finished it with her. I have to admit, it had its moments, and the Ursula Andress bikini was definitely one of them. The score was another.

We had a discussion and I found that there were more James Bond movies, so we started renting them. The ones that stood out for me were:

"Goldfinger" To me, this was the first James Bond movie. After "Goldfinger," the rest of the James Bond films took over its formula. A mini mission to start the film before credits with an epic "title song" by a female artist with a huge voice. James Bond then goes to *M* to get his mission, and then to *Q* to get his gadget weapons. Then the mission begins. We also start to see the ridiculously named "Bond Girls" *Pussy Galore* being the best...ever. I find that in some weird way, every James Bond movie since is trying to make as great a film as "Goldfinger" was.

"Thunderball" The setting for "Thunderball" is what makes this movie great. The epic underwater battles that take place with spear guns, masks, and flippers is awesome. I also enjoy one of the best cheesy one-liners ever, after Bond has killed a villain with a spear gun: "I think he got the point."

"You Only Live Twice" Yet another interesting setting, this time Japan, and there are plot points that take place in outer space. The opening sequence is quite shocking, but extremely effective. I feel too that the action in this Bond film in particular was really amped up.

"The Man with the Golden Gun" There is a lot of cool shit about this movie. First of all, the villain's name, Francisco Scaramanga. He does have a golden gun, and it has golden bullets = awesome. There are cars that turn into airplanes and one of Scaramanga's henchmen is Tattoo from Fantasy Island. There is also a duel in Scaramanga's lair...and Scaramanga is played by Saruman.

"The Spy Who Loved Me" Barbara Bach...do I need to keep writing? This film probably has the coolest open mission sequence in all of the Bond films. It is an arctic mission and there are skis, machine guns, snow machines, and a submarine that looks like an iceberg. The scale of this James Bond film is one of the largest, and that is saying a lot. There is a Lamborghini that turns into a mini submarine and a man named *Jaws* kills a shark by eating it. If that isn't sweet enough for you, I can't entertain you.

"A View to a Kill" First of all, Duran Duran has the title song, and it rocks. Second, Christopher Walken plays a very interesting "Bond villain" that is backed up by a Grace Jones that can pick men up off the ground and throw them. I love this underrated and forgotten Bond film.

...and, my favorite Bond film...

"License to Kill" I love this Bond film for a number of reasons. Number 1, it is the first Bond film I ever saw on the big screen (you always remember your first). Number 2, it breaks away from the "Goldfinger formula" that was set so many years ago. James Bond is the best man at one of his CIA Operative friend's wedding. They break from the wedding to capture the villain of the film. The Villain escapes and exacts his brutal revenge on Bond's friends, killing his new wife and subjecting his friend to a near death. Bond then has to flee from her majesty's secret service in order to get his revenge. The villain is not a "cartoon" Bond villain. Everything about him appears very real as he is a drug cartel king pin that does not suffer fools or betrayal. I feel that this is the grittiest Bond film out there, and a lot of people were not ready for this type of James Bond that would go to the lengths he had to for his revenge. Go see it.

"There are no such things as vampires, fruitcake!"

My dad *loved* "monster" horror movies.

I asked him why that was his favorite genre once and he talked about the horror movies that he watched growing up and how "pathetic" they were. Bela Lugosi's "Dracula" was the main one I remember him referring to. He remembered seeing the "bat on a string" for the first time and thinking, *ridiculous*. He was always impressed with the groundbreaking makeup and special effects that movies continued to get better at over the decades.

The first "monster" horror picture that my dad let me watch--with his supervision of course--was "Fright Night."

My dad loved this movie. I know because I remember "hearing" him watch it many times. At our old house in town when I was younger, our entertainment center was downstairs and very secluded. We had an iron, circle-descending staircase that led to the basement, making it impossible to sneak down and watch it with him.

We were able to peer over the first step and look down to see the television, but we could only watch it upside down and you had a few moments before the blood rushed to your head, creating discomfort. Not worth it.

I remember nagging my dad to watch that movie multiple times, and received the usual "no".
I found out later that one of my cousins had seen it. He

said that it wasn't that scary; that it was, "sort of funny." I told my dad this and he finally agreed to let me watch it with him (I believe I was 11 at the time--3 years after its initial release).

I was glad my dad was there to watch it with me. It freaked me out a little. For its time, the makeup and vampire special effects were amazing. The prosthetic eyes, fingers, and jaws that the actors used were original concepts in 1985 and were used in multiple horror movies that would follow thereafter.

I remember enjoying the tension of the young boy possibly being murdered by the neighbor next door. He was very vulnerable, and could not get help from anybody because vampires aren't real. It made the odds of survival seem unlikely. The police couldn't help him, his friends didn't believe him, and we are setup to be the only support that Charlie has as the viewer. What the hell are we gonna do? Oh, and the villain is a vampire that can kill three giant bouncers in less-than-a-heartbeat after 80s club dancing with Charlie's lady friend.

I found the film very entertaining and enjoyed Chris Sarandon as the villain. When a villain can scare you, but make you feel comfortable with his charm right before he attempts to strike you with a final blow...that's villainy at its finest.

When the remake with Colin Farrell came out in 2011, I went right out and saw it. I remember enjoying parts of what they did with it, but didn't enjoy it like I had the original.

*　*　*

I did a viewing of the original with some of my friends afterward and they were not impressed and felt that it didn't hold up.

I disagree. I think it holds up fine and is a movie that knew what it was making and had fun laughing along side itself. Next to "The Blues Brothers" its probably the movie that I re-watched the most with my dad over the years. Maybe that is why it is so special to me. Who knows?

I don't enjoy vampire movies in general, but I did enjoy this one. It was very different from the vampire films that I was used to. It was witty, suburban, and educational. Knowing that my dad enjoyed it so much made me want to share in that enjoyment with him...which I did and will continue to do.

"Yes, you're very smart. Shut up."

When looking for a quote for this next movie, it was going to be damn near impossible without giving it away.

I did my best.

I think this might be the most quotable movie that most people do by accident.

I remember watching this movie for the first time with my family and my older sister skipped on it as she started watching it at a friends house and did not enjoy it. She was too cool for it.

I'll have to admit, until they reached "The Cliffs of Insanity" I was on the fence. When Fezzik put on a saddle and carried three people up a rope to the top of the cliffs, I was hooked and realized I was watching an epic satire.

"The Princess Bride" is easily my favorite Rob Reiner film. That is saying a lot. He has an amazing filmography as a director. "This is Spinal Tap," "Stand By Me," "When Harry Met Sally," "Misery," "The American President," "Ghosts of Mississippi," and "Flipped," just to name a few masterpieces.

A lot of the success has to be shared with William Goldman. The author of the great novel by the same name and an amazing screenwriter himself of such classics as "Butch Cassidy & the Sundance Kid," "Stepford Wives," "All the President's Men," and

"Marathon Man," (also adapted from one of his novels) to name a few. If you haven't watched these, try and find them and give them a chance. You won't be disappointed. Some of these will appear on my list later as well.

Back to it.

I remember taking the same journey as the grandson in the picture. Not impressed at first with the love story (I was 11 years old) and the fact that Westley was killed off screen was annoying to me. But as soon as Vizzini, Inigo, and Fezzik enter the picture, the film takes off and it is memorable moment after memorable moment.

The shrieking eels, the cliffs of insanity, the fencing, the wrestling, the battle of wits, the fire swamp, the R-O-U-S's, the pit of despair, Miracle Max, storming the castle....did I miss anything? Probably.

Villains become heroes, heroes are unveiled as masterminds, magicians come out of the woodwork, and revenge is had. All in less than a 100 minutes. By the end of it, I couldn't believe that my sister didn't love it.

I did.

I mentioned how quotable it was, but the visuals in the film are amazing too from the costumes, the externals, the sets, and the props; everything was done with such precision and care.

Years later I ended up reading the novel and enjoyed the film even more after that. I caught a lot more of the dialogue during the fencing and understood it. The book equipped me with a lot of back story for the characters that gave them more depth and I got the pleasure of an "extra" ending as well.

What are your favorite quotes from this picture?

I would love to hear your thoughts.

That would make my day.

But please do....As you wish.

"In technical terminology: he's a loon."

So...after "Fright Night," my parents started loosening their grip on the R rated movie viewing guidelines that they had enforced.

One of the things that helped was the made-for-tv-edited-version of movies. I grew to hate those versions as I progressed through adulthood, but as a kid, I wanted to watch some damn movies.

We used to record them on VHS and edit out the commercials. We would hit "play/record" and when an ad popped up, we'd hit "pause." Once the ad was over, we'd hit "pause" again to continue recording. It gave us something to pay attention to during the ads. It never went as smoothly as I just described. One or more of the 3 things I'm going to describe always happened:

1. We would forget to hit pause when the movie came back on and would miss approximately 10 minutes of story until we noticed again and fixed it (then it was time for another commercial).

2. The ads ended up being so long, the VCR would auto-stop after being on pause too long and we wouldn't notice; crucial story points missed again, etc.

3. We would run out of tape on the VHS we were using; auto-stop...auto-rewind (this one always made me laugh later).

* * *

I think that our first experiment with this disaster (that we continued to do--regardless) was "The Terminator."

People don't remember what a big deal that first movie was. Everyone talks about the sequel, deservedly, but for its time, "The Terminator" was an amazing story told by a special effects master that would become one of the greatest directors of the Hollywood blockbuster of all time.

For me, it was the story that carried the film. Within the first 30 minutes, you're engaged, but you are not sure what is going on other than knowing that a former body builder is going around L. A. killing Sarah Connors from the phone book in order.

It's when the 3rd and final Sarah Connor is saved by another shady character on the run from the police that we get the real story and start to get invested.

The movie was commended for its amazing special effects, prosthetic makeup, animation, spectacle explosions, and action sequences.

For me though, it was always those moments in between the action with Kyle Reese and Sarah Connor that carried the story. It gave the audience a reprieve from all of the action and violence and helped deliver the plot elements that were necessary to get us up to speed and offer that "human" element (pun...I know). It also helped create a "suspense payoff" in a way as they both showed us how vulnerable they really were against this juggernaut cyborg from the future. Whenever he was within 50 yards of them, you thought they were going to die. The film will be labeled as Science Fiction, but James Cameron was very effective at using horror violence as a suspense tactic to put the viewer at unrest.

I feel that "The Terminator" was a "light bulb" moment for me. The movie was out for about four years before I finally got to see it for the first time. Everyone that had been talking about it would mention the action and the violence, but I didn't really get a sense of the premise or the story until I viewed it.

When Reese talks to Sarah in the car that they are trying to jack about her son and why she has to live--that is the moment I think about and remember how important a story is in film. Put as many cyborg, serial killer, monsters in a movie that you want, if you don't have a purpose for them, you just have another survival story, but if the fate of mankind depends on these moments that we are viewing, we're going to be captivated; very simple and effective writing/storytelling that can make a decent sci-fi action thriller great.

"I'd go with you but-"..."I know, there's a problem with your face."

Sometimes movies get caught taking themselves too seriously. Every poorly written movie that can't throw a little giggle at itself--hell, even wink a little--is committing cinema suicide. Tone plays such a crucial part in any story being told. When you have a pitch about a 2000 year old villain that needs the blood of a certain bride to give him his powers back to rule the entire world and he uses Rain, Thunder, and Lightning (all characters played by men) to do his bidding; brother, that movie better know that it should laugh at itself or you will get laughed right out of your pitch meeting. Especially if this movie is supposed to occur in a modern day Chinatown.

Enter Jack Burton. If Dirty Harry ever had a son, Jack Burton was his rebellious teenager.

Played by Kurt Russell, Jack is the "lead" in "Big Trouble in Little China." I can't imagine any other person playing Jack with the necessary restraint at times that Russell was able to pull off. He is a larger than life character, that unfortunately only had the opportunity to be contained in a 2 hour movie. No one was brave enough to try and duplicate his dialogue for a sequel or spin-off for that matter. I can't say that I blame them. He's the kind of lovable loser, that is able to stumble his way through to a victory over the dark lords he faces in this cult classic. It doesn't hurt that he appears as the sidekick to Wang Chi ([Dennis Dun](#)) who has the ability to do the same amazing, super-human/acrobatic flights through the air as Rain, Thunder, and Lightning.

* * *

Jack is a truck driver that is friends with Wang. Wang is awaiting the arrival of his future bride so that they can get married and live happily. Our villain, Lo Pan (played by the ever unforgettable [James Hong](#)) interferes as Wang's Bride to be is the only woman that can break the curse holding Lo Pan back from his goal of world domination.

Jack's semi goes missing and gets him involved at length, much like Wang with his bride to be. There are many "Kung Fu Movie" action set pieces, along with a number of damsel's in distress ([Kim Cattrall](#) being one of them along with Wang's bride to be), monsters, and old Chinese wizards too. If you hear all of that and think that this sounds ridiculous, I'm here to tell you that it is and the movie knows it--very crucial. This is a very entertaining film. There are elements of horror, action/adventure and above all, comedy. [John Carpenter](#) was known for his suspense and horror pictures ("[Halloween](#)," "[The Thing](#)," "[Christine](#)," "[Escape from New York](#)"). I feel that because of his ability to gel all of the different genres that he was familiar with together and create a film that laughs at itself, he delivered a very weird sort of masterpiece that finally found a following on home video. My dad loved it. My mom left the room after the first scene.

"Well, then the law's crazy."

This next one was another in a list of many that I saw the first time as a made for television movie a.k.a. blood-violence and curse words dubbed out.

Being that it was made in 1971, there wasn't a whole lot that they had to leave out.

I remember a well dressed tall man that noticed a lot of other things that everyone else didn't. A car parked out in front of a bank--still running, for an uncomfortable period of time. Like a prophet, there are shots fired at the bank and Harry, who wanted to enjoy his early afternoon dinner, is instead forced into action.

He is able to resolve the "situation" with multiple casualties on the other side. At the tail-end of that scene, the writers made Clint Eastwood a film icon.

I always wondered what it would be like to write something that made an actor a film legend. Did Fink, Fink, & Riesner know that they were writing dialogue that would make some actor's words and public perception timeless? My guess is "no." They probably just did what the rest of us do. Thought of things that needed to be said, and bled them out onto the page.

I remember thinking that if the film had ended after that first sequence at the bank heist after his amazing monologue, it'd been a perfect film. It didn't end there...it got better.

* * *

The story really starts to unfold when Harry starts to hunt down a known female child murderer. Enter, "Killer." That's literally the character name on the cast sheet.

Fitting.

[Andrew Robinson](#) was perfect casting. Nobody could forget those "crazy blue eyes." He was so good, Hollywood only allowed him to play television villains and side street-hoods until he finally found a role as Garak on "[Deep Space Nine](#)" in the 90s (22 years later). Along with the eyes, Robinson carried the smarmy mannerisms and a sniveling voice that spews "evil villain." With someone as vile as this, you'd think there could be only one showdown between these two larger than life characters. Oh no, there's two epic showdowns in one stoic film; both memorable for different reasons.

This was one of the first "cop" movies I had been exposed to. There have been many that have tried to duplicate it on some level, but have failed. The real reason: Clint Eastwood can't be in every cop movie. I really feel like some part of America has always enjoyed "Dirty Harry" and some part always will. He is a very simple character: do what is right, do what is necessary--scumbags need to die. This isn't the type of movie that you watch when you need to study the intricate details of the theme, tone, and plot structure (although a lot of people that want to make a good "cop" movie could learn from analyzing this film); but it is a great film to "escape" into when you are ready for a simple good vs. evil scenario in which good pummels evil's ass at every turn of the corner.

* * *

The good guy *should* win, right?

> "Yes. I, too, like him very much. It's very hard not to."

My parents are not big fans of Eddie Murphy.

Every kid in the 80s was.

I didn't get many chances to watch Eddie Murphy in his early career because of the language content of his movies. All of my friends were allowed to and talked about it at school. I was jealous and begged my parents, but they stood strong. Years later--*clears throat*--YEARS LATER, I appreciated that.

There was just one movie that fell through the cracks.

It's the story of a man that spends his life finding children that are missing. A woman sees him on a local television show in LA announcing the latest missing child that he is searching for. The woman seeks him out and approaches him for some work. He reluctantly takes the job and sets off on an unexpected investigation/adventure that takes him all around the world and back.

His favorite phrase, "....I'm gonna bust yo ass!"

"The Golden Child" was another eclectic movie. There was obvious humor, Eddie Murphy was in it. There were exotic locations, fantastical villains, a bad ass karate-chopping heroine, dragons, gargoyles, and of course magic.

* * *

My parents were reluctant. After all, it did have that "filthy" Eddie Murphy in it. So they had to screen it of course. They were only willing to even screen it after they heard me and my cousins talking about it. My cousins had seen it and enjoyed it. My mom started asking them questions:

"Was there a lot of swearing in it?"

"No."

"Was there any sex in it?"

"No."

"Was there a lot of violence?"

"Not a lot."

"Was there nudity?"

"What's that?"

We found out what that meant and there was none of that in it either (unless you count the topless dragon).

When I watched it, I found it very unexpected. I didn't just enjoy it because I finally got to see an Eddie Murphy movie. I actually enjoyed the story, the characters, the action, and the humor was just a bonus. My favorite scenes are the ones that involve Eddie Murphy and Charles Dance (you know, Tyrion's dad).

Dance is excellent at playing a man that is built to

frighten you. Eddie Murphy is excellent at playing over-confident. As an audience, we're aware of how dangerous Dance is. We have seen that he is not human, that he can appear, murder, and be gone. Murphy is not in on that trick and treats Dance like he is just another man. This adds tension for us when we see Murphy antagonize him. We enjoy the humor in those scenes, but we worry for the well being of Murphy as well.

In the end, I decided to watch this movie more than the one time and tried to memorize all of the funny scenes so that I could talk with my friends about them at school.

I did that...my Eddie Murphy impression leaves something to be desired.

"Who are those guys?"

I'll hit a John Wayne series later...today is going to be a different western.

Charming-villain-heroes.

I remember watching this movie with my mother on VHS for the first time and she was so excited to get it started. I sat beside her and noticed her giddy gestures right before her favorite scenes unfolded in front of us on the television.

From the "knife fight" at the beginning to the "dynamite" on the safe. From the chase through the wilderness to the free fall into the river. From the bank montages in Bolivia to the final showdown that fades to black and white.

"Butch Cassidy and the Sundance Kid" was my first exposure to Robert Redford and Paul Newman. After I saw this, I immediately made my mom rent "The Sting." (She told me about it. She could rent it. I didn't have to twist her arm. We can talk about "The Sting" later.)

I had to admit, I was shocked--AT FIRST--that my mother was rooting for these bank robbers. After about 10 minutes, that wore off and I couldn't wait to see Newman and Redford interact on screen in each upcoming scene. The chemistry that those two actors displayed in the entirety of that film is unlike any I have seen two actors share together on film and has never been duplicated to such perfection. In a matter of seconds, we believe these two know each other better than they know themselves. Quite honestly, it carried the picture. The story is very simple; but the correct acting can make any simple story seem special.

Don't get me wrong. I love William Goldman, and he wrote some good lines; but without the delivery of Redford and Newman, I don't know that this film gets the credit that it deserves over the years. The delivery is crucial as well as the feeling of back story that we get without knowing any of their past. They make it very easy for us to believe that these two have known each other their entire lives; with the use of subtle gestures, giggles, and facial expressions. A little says a lot between these two, especially in this film.

I have multiple favorite scenes, but I will always hold the "wilderness chase to the river drop" as the best set of sequences. It carries our attention through a very crucial time in the film where we could check out if needed, but it is able to keep us captivated with drama, suspense, and eventually--humor.

Is this the best western ever made?

Not in my book. It may not even be top 5, but it is a very entertaining story because of these two actors and their ability to convey a very "real" relationship.

I always liked to ask people, "Do you think you're Sundance or Cassidy?"

It was a barometer I used to judge how people thought of themselves. I had to stop using it after the 90s as I started being around more and more people that had never seen it, which is a shame. I had a lot of fun conversations with people about that one.

I'm definitely Sundance....I don't know if that's good or bad.

"I think there's just a couple o' guys up there and this asshole's one of 'em!"

This is one of my most favorite underrated films of all time.

I say underrated because it did not do well at the box office (historic flop). It also never really got a chance to be too successful at VHS as that was a rather new media still in 1985--plus they had to deal with the likes of "Out of Africa," "The Color Purple," "Kiss of the Spider Woman," "Prizzi's Honor," "Witness," "Runaway Train," "Cocoon," "Jagged Edge," "Ran," "Back to the Future," "Ladyhawke," and oh yeah, "White Nights."

I think this was the first Western I saw that didn't have John Wayne in it.

I'm going to list the cast right now and you see if you can guess the film--those of you that can, already know the film I'm talking about, most likely:

Kevin Kline

Scott Glenn

Kevin Costner (young)

Danny Glover

John Cleese

* * *

Rosanna Arquette

Linda Hunt

Brian Dennehy

and a very brief Jeff Goldblum

"Silverado" was a movie that knew what was popular about Westerns (guns, horses, chases through the open range, cattle stampedes, lovable loser cowboys, big rifles, fires, churches, and nasty, nasty villains).

Right out of the gate before the "fade in" from black we hear a gunshot. Our hero Emmett (played by the silent and deadly Scott Glenn) leaps into action half asleep and defends his ground against two villains that attempt to kill him in an ambush as he sleeps. If you weren't paying attention through the credit role, you are now.

The film starts out as a Western "road picture" as we watch Emmett travel through the frontier meeting many different people along the way. He runs into one of my favorite cowboys, Paden--played brilliantly by the underrated Kevin Kline laying near death in the desert in nothing but his red long underwear.

We get to meet Emmett through Paden and Paden through Emmett over their conversations and join them as they travel from town to town.

The two of them end up rescuing Emmett's rowdy younger brother Jake (young Costner) from a very snooty little town, and make friends with a fourth man along the way in Mal--Danny Glover. With their new formed posse they help rescue a wagon train (heading to Silverado) from marauders, and decide to finish the trip with them. Jake and Emmett have family there, along with Mal who has a kid sister that lives and works there.

Lawrence Kasdan has done an amazing job keeping us engaged on the trek to Silverado, and then the storytelling starts and we are drawn into the past relationships and how they will effect the future of the town.

Brian Dennehy enters onto screen as the notorious Cobb that Paden has been talking about here and there for most of the journey. Dennehy owns this part better than any other he has portrayed on film. I mean that as a compliment as he is an amazing, sometimes forgotten actor. He is the perfect kind of villain. He seems charming at first and wants to help. He laughs and has a good time, and then in seconds he shows his ruthlessness and we are at the edge of our seat every time he steps into frame.

Kasdan is a master at telling many stories in one film that conclude at the climax. He has to be one of the greatest writers that Hollywood has put out. "The Empire Strikes Back," "Raiders of the Lost Ark," "Body Heat," "Return of the Jedi," "The Big Chill," "Silverado," "The Accidental Tourist," and "Grand Canyon," to name a few--all of which I love. I'd say if you haven't seen "Silverado" and "Body Heat," they should be the next two movies you seek out.

* * *

At the end of the day, this movie is a testosterone filled adventure that all boys love. There are plenty of shootouts, but there is also plenty of very well written dialogue. The scenes between Linda Hunt and Kline are some of my favorite in the film and I get excited to watch those two across from each other every time I see it.

In the end, we have a true western, with very real actors carrying a great formula that keeps us in our seats and delivers what we want.

> "...death is listening, and will take the first man that screams."

My dad, like many people, loved the Mel Gibson of the early 80s.

He was energetic, showed great charisma, and seemed to enjoy the material that he chose to perform in regardless of its worth/popularity.

Enter "Mad Max." These were some of the first films I remember my dad renting after we got our VCR. I didn't really get to see "Mad Max" or "Mad Max 2: The Road Warrior." I recall flashes of sounds and pictures as I walked through the room to go outside as I was not allowed to watch those movies yet. There were a lot of people in black leather, driving large vehicles, explosions, car chases, and "traffic accidents" of an interstate-pile-up-persuasion. That is just from brief glimpses, on a walk-through or two...(okay 6).

A few years after the release, my dad rented "Mad Max: Beyond Thunderdome" and I was allowed to watch it this time. When compared to the other two films, this one was WAY different in scope. The costuming was very similar, and I'd say that's about it. The locations were well crafted, the open landscape desert visuals were "Lawrence of Arabia" breathtaking, and the performances were what was necessary to move the story--big and BIGGER!

For those of you that weren't around for Tina Turner in the 80s, she was something more than a rock star. She was a cross between a legend like Elvis and a POP STAR like Michael Jackson. So when she decided to take up acting, everyone was like, "Makes sense...."

I write this like it was her first acting endeavor. It wasn't...but it's the one that she will be remembered for, as it should be.

Gibson also flashed a new look that he carried into the early 90s. His long shaggy hair. Everyone was used to the clean-cut, sexy blue-eyed ass kicker from the earlier films. This one was a new Max. Still the ass kicker, wiser, yet vulnerable in a weird way. He starts off in the picture getting mugged in the middle of the desert and being left for dead.

Enter the story and the metaphors and you have a picture that I think [George Miller](#) and [George Ogilvie](#) couldn't wait to start telling.

Now don't get me wrong, if you're looking for an intricate plot, this is not the picture for you. If you want a very well acted action/adventure that takes you to many different places in a short amount of time with amazing stunts, set pieces, and visuals (costumes, sets, props, locations, etc.) this is definitely the picture for you; and in my meager opinion--very underrated and sometimes forgotten.

Years later I sat down with my dad to do a marathon of the three movies. It was great to relax and talk through these movies together. It was something that we always enjoyed doing when we had the time to catch up. For what they were worth, the first two films were well crafted for low budget action films that used the Australian landscape as a vivid backdrop. Thunderdome stood out, however, apart from the other pictures. It was the third child that exceeded expectations tenfold and graduated from the Ivy Leagues.

It's amazing to me what can be done with a decent story when you have the backing from a large studio for your third installment.

My dad and I never said it out loud specifically to each other, but we could tell that the love and care that was put into the third picture was much needed for the franchise, and delivered way better than anyone could have imagined.

Go see it. I think you'll be pleasantly surprised...I hope.

> "I would rather be with the people of this town than with the finest people in the world."

Oh Daryl Hannah....

My how glorious she was--to look at.

Perfect casting for this film. After her "awesome bottom" scenes in "Splash" every man and boy that watched her, lusted after her. She had to be the woman that needs to capture the affection of C. D. Bales and the rest of the small town in "Roxanne."

I remember watching this with my mom and dad in the summer time. I knew it was summer because we were able to start and finish the whole movie without going to bed at 8pm for school the next day half way through the movie.

I hated when that happened. This is one of the first movies I remember watching in its entirety with my parents after we had our VCR.

I give credit to Hannah, equal credit should be given to Rick Rossovich.

He takes on the role of Chris, the hunky new fireman that is everything but smooth with the women, in a friendly/reckless manner that is both pitiful and charming for the viewer. His bumbling and comedic timing when he is showing signs of nerves around Roxanne for the first time is priceless. How many of us have felt that same way around beautiful women? How many of us have used a "faulty" faucet in the boys bathroom and got water all over our pants? (Yes, I did dammit--I couldn't escape out a window like Chris though, I was at school and had to get back to class....I DON'T WANT TO TALK ABOUT IT)

Steve Martin as C. D. Bales, the local fire chief, is amazing as always. People generally remember the bar scene in which he defends his own honor by taking jabs at his physical "deformity," making his antagonist look like a foolish ass. Great scene....deserves the accolades that it has gotten over the years...but, it is not my favorite scene.

I love the scene where Chris is attempting to woo Roxanne while wearing an Elmer Fudd hat to cover up the earpiece that C. D. is using to communicate with him by feeding the lines that Roxanne will want to hear as C. D. is camped out in a surveillance van. Needless to say there are technical problems, hilarious facial expressions for all involved, and laugh out loud comedy ensues.

Martin also takes advantage of his physical comedy skills in this picture in a very controlled and acrobatic manner in almost every scene that he is in.

The drama that all of the actors are asked to convey is genuine as well. I appreciated the misunderstandings, the longing, and the discomfort of watching someone else be with the woman that you love so dearly.

* * *

In the end, this is a comedy of sorts, but it is a great modernization of an old story.

When I first saw this, I had never heard of "Cyrano de Bergerac." My mother explained to me later that it was an adaptation of that play. I never had any interest to read or watch a different version after my first viewing of this film.

I still feel that way.

"I KNOW what a 'BURRITO' is!"

You don't realize until way later that you have discovered a movie star for the first time. There were many not yet discovered in this film that would be discovered later. The person I remember wanting to see more of, was Nic Cage.

Don't get me wrong. I had seen Cage perform in other movies that I loved him in (briefly in "Rumble Fish" and again briefly in "Fast Times at Ridgemont High"), but after watching "Peggy Sue Got Married" I wanted to see even more.

To boot, Kathleen Turner was in it. My God...I loved her.

I'll get to that, just give me a sec to talk about my man-crush on young Nic...

His voice inflection alone in this movie is worth a viewing. He is also a key component in a "doo wop" group that features an extremely young Jim Carrey who had an opportunity (however brief) to show off his comedic talent in the limited amount of time he has on screen. If you decide to take a viewing, watch for him. Nic, Jim, and the other guys *CAN* really sing; quite impressive. I feel that this was that early role that Nic Cage took advantage of and put himself ALL IN and showed what he "*wanted*" to do as opposed to what he "*could*" do. It didn't hurt that his uncle was the director.

At the end of the day, the story is remarkable and

inventive.

At her 20 year reunion, Peggy Sue (Turner--obviously) faints and wakes up in her old life back in high school. We know very little about her current circumstances--only that her marriage to her high school sweetheart Charlie (Cage--again, obviously) is over and ended on very heartbreaking terms--all of which we piece together with subtle bits of dialogue from conversations she has with her daughter (played by a yet to be discovered Helen Hunt--there's more where that came from).

Peggy Sue obviously remembers everything of her future now and wants to make major changes to her life based on what she has learned.

Who the hell wouldn't want to do this? I have yet to meet anyone that wouldn't...that whole, "Youth is wasted on the *youth*" notion.

I remember learning so much about the culture that Peggy Sue (and my mom) grew up in. There are very many 1960s pop culture references. Peggy Sue would say something, I'd ask mom to pause it and explain. She did. It was a lot of fun, not just to experience a great story, but to learn about the time period my mom grew up in was interesting and exciting for me too.

Watching Cage's Charlie do an emotional tango with Turner's Peggy Sue is entertaining on a comedic level, while it builds into a very dramatic waltz when the stakes are at their highest toward the climax of the film.

Definitely worth a viewing, and thankfully, Charlie never

took Peggy up on her offer to sing "She Loves You" for the first time. The *"Yeah, Yeah, Yeahs,"* can continue to be as timeless as they are now.

That last little bit kind of dares you to watch this movie. I hope you catch the reference. It's by far my favorite 1960s pop culture mention in the movie and I don't think I'll ever be able to forget it.

"Hey, that's no fair. The building guy lived."

I'll just say it...I miss Martin Riggs.

Come on...crazy eyes, flaring nostrils, tobacco breath, and don't forget the flowing locks of that smooth lion's mane mullet that only Mel could pull off. That character was priceless.

My first experience with him was again under the influence of "edited for television." I didn't care. That version still had enough car chases, gunfights, and explosions. I also found it fun to try and pick out which phrases were really curse words from the original version. It wasn't that hard; poor dubbing drew attention to it. I'm sure someone out there thinks they're very clever with the different phrases they came up with to dub-in alternately; but even at 10 years old I knew what they were saying.

I think everyone knew it wasn't a real "firing" gun.

I miss Murtaugh too. Over the hill, on his last legs, he's still got game, but he hates running, shooting and yelling. He just wants to bring people in, question them, and arrest bigger bad guys.

When we first meet Riggs, we're not sure what to think of him. He looks like another junky trying to score some "H" on the street, when he lays a bomb of a badge on the table and we're all in as viewers from that point forward (I personally was "all in" during that shootout at that Christmas tree lot when Riggs decides to wheel-barrel role on the ground while dodging returning fire and plugging about six bullets from his Beretta into the drug dealer trying to kill him).

Emotionally, Riggs isn't doing well as he appears to have a death wish while on the job and--in his private life--he teeters on swallowing a hollow-point bullet through the back of his head day-to-day.

Enter Murtaugh:

A family man that's looking forward to getting "off the street" soon.

Of course he's the perfect man to help keep Riggs focused on the work.

Riggs is the perfect man to help Murtaugh keep up his energy for the "job."

I know that I have set this up as a cliche buddy cop movie, but at the time of it's making, buddy cop movies weren't a cliche yet and even if they were, they weren't as good as "Lethal Weapon." For me, this is the gold standard "buddy cop" movie that the rest of them are measured by.

Oh, and there is a plot. A good one, and I don't want to give too many details away.

Just know this, one of--what I feel--the greatest underrated and forgotten actors plays a stone-cold-killer of a villain in this movie.

* * *

Now, when I say his name, I know you'll chuckle. He has made himself quite a caricature at this point, but at one time--he was an amazing actor in the late 70s through the 80s. I don't know what happened to Gary Busey (go ahead, I know you want to laugh) but if you take a look at his filmography, he had some amazing roles in: "The Buddy Holly Story," "The Bear (as Paul "The Bear" W. Bryant)," "Silver Bullet," "Let's Get Harry," "Lethal Weapon," and later "Point Break."

He really stepped out of himself in this role as a very level, silent killer that could frighten anyone just by stepping into the room.

All in all, we do watch this film for it's central relationship. We want Murtaugh to live because he has put in his time over the years and we meet his beautiful, thriving family. We especially want Murtaugh to be the man that can bring some form of peace to Riggs and keep him alive.

We see Riggs grow as the protector, giving him a sense of purpose when the stakes are at their highest. We also see that Murtaugh has PLENTY left in the tank, and he wouldn't even know that it was always there stirring inside of him, waiting to overflow, if Riggs wasn't dropped into his life.

Call it another "buddy cop" movie if you want....

To me, it's the first "buddy cop" movie that I ever saw and have ever seen.

"Please, they're dead. It's a little late to be neurotic."

I'm going to write a post on my favorite costume that I wore on Halloween growing up. *Pssssssst--it's from a movie.*

My mom took one of those "bald caps," threaded some white yarn through the top and back all around it; I put on some white paint all over my face, neck and hands, and around my eyes--black paint.

I wish I had a picture. I'd totally post it side-by-side with the real character...it was a little harder to take pictures in the 80s; apologies.

I was obsessed with this character in junior high, and I couldn't wait for his scenes whenever I re-watched the movie.

The film [opens](#) with a tracking shot over the town that the story takes place in. At least we think it is a town...

At the end of the tracking shot--at the house at the end of the road--a rather large spider climbs over the miniature model of the home that the majority of the story takes place in.

We meet a younger married couple that is having an average weekend day as they head into town to run a few errands. They have a car accident on the bridge while trying to avoid a dog.

* * *

Cut to the two of them entering their home, drenched.

They start to notice that things are stranger and notice a "handbook" sitting on an end table. We, along with the couple, soon learn that they did not survive the car accident on the bridge and are now a part of a very bizarre afterlife.

This film was my second exposure to Tim Burton's work. I saw "Pee Wee's Big Adventure" when I was in elementary school and I laughed, but the visuals didn't stick with me like they did from "Beetlejuice."

Not only are our protagonists, dead, their beautiful home was purchased by people that want to destroy it and make it their own. They soon learn that the only thing they can do to defend themselves and their home is to become ghosts, with which they learn that they are not good at that--remotely.

Enter Betelgeuse.

This has to be my favorite Michael Keaton character. I'd be surprised if he is even actually on film 30 minutes in this entire 92 minute movie. The scenes we all remember and love are his, however. I get the sense that Burton gave him the freedom to be the actor that he can be at times and this is the result of the best that Michael Keaton can be. He is funny, indecent, disgusting, and frightening from one second to the next. His voice changes and delivery are amazing. He also has many opportunities where he displays his physical humor as well (his dance in front of the whorehouse is unforgettable--can't decide if that's good or bad...)

It's unfortunate that it takes approximately one hour for him to get onscreen. Once he is on, that's all we want to see. I think that I have everyone of his lines memorized.

I felt that a lot of the visuals (sets, props, costumes, makeup, etc.) are very "Dr. Seussian" in terms of the odd angles and skewed views. It is a staple in Burton's films moving forward.
It is also the film where I fell in love with Winona Ryder for a time. I remembered her from Lucas," I couldn't forget about her after "Beetlejuice."

Like "Ghostbusters," this movie had many different elements working for it. Humor, drama, terror, and creativity. I felt the tone of the picture was true from the point of the spider crawling on the home, until we see the ghosts of the football players dancing to "Jump in the Line (Shake Senora)" on the stairs behind Lydia.

Who doesn't want to float in the air while listening to Harry Belafonte?

"Would you like a nightcap?"-"No, thank you, I don't wear them."

I have not been shy about explaining how I was deprived growing up. Being sheltered from certain viewership helped me be the happy little naive kid that believed in Santa until he was 6 (it would've been longer but my cousin was an asshole and spilled the beans-not realizing everybody hates the pretentious kid that does that).

Knowing this, my parents allowed me to watch "The Naked Gun" with them.

I have to admit, during the first viewing, I did not get a lot of the jokes. I laughed at the funny faces and the slapstick the first time around.

Thank God for public schools.

It was there that I learned from my friends the adult, inside to a lot of the jokes that were in the movie. After talking to them at school, I tried to think of someone that I could watch it with that could explain things quickly along the way....had to be my cousins.

I sat down with them and turned it on. They had seen it once before, so they knew what was coming and could explain things to me.

I feel like "The Naked Gun" was my first exposure to what could be considered an all out farce. I had not seen "Airplane!" or "Caddyshack" yet (I love both of those FYI) and my parents felt at eleven I still wasn't ready for those movies.

They compromised with this one and I'm glad they did.

I remember afterwards thinking that my parents had great poker faces through some of the "raunchier" jokes. Normally my mom would give a judgmental, disgusted gasp through those parts. I think she knew those parts would go over my head so she didn't want to give me any ideas and she hoped I wouldn't ask. Now that I think about it, she probably didn't have much time to enjoy a movie while she watched one with me. Hmmmm. Never thought about that. No wonder they didn't like watching anything over "G" rated with us until we were teenagers.

At the end of the day, "The Naked Gun" introduced me to Leslie Nielsen. I rented as many movies as he had put out after I saw this. I liked his comedies. It was hard to take him seriously in the older dramas that he did when he was younger. He had found his niche and thankfully stuck to it.

I love his scenes with Priscilla Presley. Making light of soap opera melodrama is not an easy thing to pull off. Those two made it look so easy.

Nielsen to me was like Will Farrell. A little went a long way with him, and he could make you laugh just by entering a room and looking around.

I feel like I can mention some two word phrases--the second word being "scene"--and it will bring back moments from this film. I'll start off with some easy ones:

the "queen scene"

the "umpire scene"

the "condom scene"

the "wheelchair scene"

the "clothesline scene" (Remember? The one on the beach?)

When I say these phrases, I smirk.

Again, thank God for public school. I might have never gotten the beaver joke.

"Get me Bruce Lee!"-"Bruce Lee is dead."-"Then get his brother!"

So I feel I've written about some "cult classics." I think it's fair to say that "Fright Night" and "Big Trouble in Little China" are what can be considered "cult classics." For the definition, I turned to the most reliable source for accurate definitions--UD, baby. Urban Dictionary is NEVER wrong. I like all 3 definitions. I'm going to list them, not in any particular order (maybe):

cult classic

Something that's really hip with a select group of people.

Pretty basic. Cut-and-dry. Gets right to the point. I like it.

The next one is really fun if you read it with an English Accent in your head.

cult classic

A popular piece of work, generally a movie, which has gained a large following. This following has most likely been around for at least a few years, except for cases of an 'instant cult classic,' in which a movie gains instant fame which remains for decades to come.

Not bad. More detail. A very specific explanation with an example of another type of the same noun. Good stuff.

cult classic

A movie that is weird as fuck.

That's gotta be the best, right?

This next movie that I have chosen has to be the "cultiest" of cults. Some of you are going to be annoyed that I chose this and will refuse to continue reading after I give you the title. Some of you are going to hear the title, hit your head on the ceiling and yell, "Fuck yeah!"

Isn't that how cult classics work? You love 'em or you hate 'em. Gray? Come on.

I like to ask people, "Who's an underrated bad ass of films in the 80s?" I think the word underrated makes it an interesting question. If you just ask pure bad ass, people will throw out [Arnold](#) and [Sly](#) and [Dolph](#)...but underrated adds some dimension. Its not supposed to be the ones that pop right in there. For me, it will always be Rutger Hauer.

Now I know I already mancrushed on him when I wrote about "Ladyhawke," but hear me out.
Arnold, and Sly for the most part were the "good guys." Hell, Arnold was a villain in "[The Terminator](#)" and in the sequel he was the hero (not to mention in each one in that series following--when he was cast). Name a movie where Sly played a villain ("[Oscar](#)" doesn't count). Dolph, like Arnold, started as a villain, but was cast as an action hero bad ass after that until "[Universal Soldier](#)" when he fell off the face of the earth.

* * *

Get to the point asshole.

My point is that Rutger was able to do multiple bad ass roles on both sides of the spectrum. He could play a villain you never wanted to walk across the street from and a hero that could knock you out with his piercing gaze.

Let's examine his list:

villain = "Nighthawks (Sly's the hero...coincidence?)" "Blade Runner" and "The Hitcher"

hero = "The Osterman Weekend" of course "Ladyhawke" "Wanted: Dead or Alive" and....."Blind Fury"

Yes, the best "cult classic" for last, "Blind Fury." I freaking love this ridiculous movie. Why? Because Rutger Hauer made me believe he could be a blind bad ass!

I know, after finally building up to what I normally write for one post, I get to the movie...sorry.

Outside of Rutger Hauer becoming a "Zatoichi" style bad ass (which I have *clearly* established), here's what you need to know:

The film features Randall "Tex" Cobb as Slag. Cobb is one of my favorite typecast, villain actors of the 80s. He is lights out as the antagonist in this movie, and he gets an epic Darth Maul demise. Cobb was used as the Featured Image for my post on The Golden Child" and he was also in Raising Arizona" which will receive a chapter from me as well.

There are creative action sequences from beginning to end, and....

...the hero only knows how to use a sword...because he's blind.

Go see it.

You might regret it, you might not = essence of "cult classic."

"Well factually, the..."

Outside of Quentin Tarantino right now, are there writers that enjoy all that there is about the "American-English" language more than Joel and Ethan Coen?

I will admit, I didn't really have a clear understanding for their genius with writing on my first viewings, but they eventually won me over and have become one on a short list of my favorite American Filmmakers.

I wasn't ready for "Raising Arizona" the first time I'd seen it, mainly because it was unlike any comedy I had ever seen before. I feel that some works of genius are rewarded later. This film definitely falls into that category.

My mom and I watched it together, and we had a difficult time concentrating on the dialogue because we were so involved in watching Nicholas Cage, Holly Hunter, John Goodman, William Forsythe, and Randall "Tex" Cobb display their physical talents. The hair and makeup people for Nicholas Cage did not get paid enough money.

This is a movie that was packed with criminals, prison breaks, kidnappings, bounty hunters, car chases, shoot outs, and explosions...did I mention that it's a comedy?

The premise alone makes me giggle.

Our convict, H. I. "You can call me Hi" McDunnough (Cage) meets our cop Ed "short for Edwina" (Hunter) as he is being booked. She (Ed) takes his (Hi's) mug shots. This extremely odd couple decides to get married and later finds that they cannot conceive children. *Hi* decides to take matters into his own hands instead of waiting for the adoption process to work and kidnaps the 7th child of a wealthy furniture store mogul, Nathan Arizona. Hence, "Raising Arizona".

Prior to watching this, my mom and I made guesses based on the title as to what the movie could be about.

"Are they going to make mountains in the Arizona desert?"

"Is Arizona going to float off into space?"

There was none of that in this movie....maybe that is why we were disappointed at first....hmm.

I don't think I will ever be able to forget the "Huggies robbery" sequence. I remember not being able to stop laughing from the moment he slid his panty hose over his head, until he reached out the door of the moving car and picked up the diapers on the road without stopping the car. I have a smile that is stretching across my face as I remember and write about it.

In the end, as many Coen Brother films were in the 80s and early 90s, this movie was ahead of it's time and can now be appreciated for what it is. An original comedy that the talent lost themselves inside of.

It was this movie that gave us a heads up for "Barton Fink" "Fargo" "The Big Lebowski" "No Country for Old

Men" and the better "True Grit"...and I left a lot of REALLY great films out, because "factually" I want you to research all of them and get to love them for the first time.

"You insignificant little pipsqueak, I'm in charge here!"

It's no surprise to anyone that I am drawn to movies with lovable losers.

The greatest is "Lucas."

I also like:

Mikey from "The Goonies"

Schmendrick from "The Last Unicorn"

Gaston from "Ladyhawke"

All of the characters in "Explorers" (well maybe not Darren)

Scott Howard from "Teen Wolf"

I'm sure I've left out a few and you get the point. The lovable loser from the next film is pathetic to the point of pity, but he becomes a man of action. The transformation is so believable and from one of the most unlikely actors to hit the screen. Martin Short's Jack Putter in "Innerspace" is definitely a top five lovable loser, all time. He tape records (that was done on a VCR in the 80s for all of you Millennials out there) game shows while he is at his day job at a grocery store. He will sometimes re-watch them more than once. He is a hypochondriac and displays high anxiety symptoms. He is in for one hell of a weekend.

* * *

I remember watching "Fantastic Voyage" with my mother when I was much younger. It was made twenty years earlier than this film and shared a lot of the same premise. In that film, a very important politician has a stroke, and a team of scientists shrink themselves into a capsule that they can then maneuver while riding around inside of his body to find the disease that they will need to destroy. When I was young, it was great! It eventually ended up being extremely campy after my first viewing of "Innerspace."

I'm going to take a line from Inigo Montoya, "Let me explain....no, there is too much, let me sum up."

Dennis Quaid as Lt. Tuck Pendleton gets involved in an experiment to test a shrinking technology and agrees to be shrunk while inside a capsule and be injected into a rabbit while in a lab. The villains of the film attempt to steal the technology in the middle of this process, there is a chase, and Pendleton ends up getting injected into Jack Putter's ass. It is now up to Jack to help keep Pendleton alive...and Pendleton becomes the voice inside of Jack, literally, of reason, courage, and wisdom.

What a great story.

Throw in some groundbreaking special effects, amazing action sequences, and a lot of suspense and you have a very entertaining 120 minutes.

Another notable performance was Robert Picardo as "The Cowboy." Picardo is most famous for his role as "the Doctor" on Star Trek: Voyager. He is an amazing character actor and has had consistent work in Hollywood for a very long time playing henchmen, slobs, wimps, and geeks. He had the difficult task of giving us a monstrous character with a few minutes of screen time, so that Jack would have enough personality to go on in order to disguise himself and pull off his role as an impostor "Cowboy."

Picardo delivers.

In the end, I love watching Jack's slow build of confidence throughout the film. The screenwriters Jeffrey Boam and Skip Proser gave Martin Short just enough moments to be, well...Martin Short, but also wrote a character that they could bring back down to earth in order to become the necessary man of action. Director Joe Dante deserves credit for helping to contain Short from making too many scenes slapstick and unbelievable.

I feel the result of all their hard work was an entertaining and exciting job well done.

"Shut up, Baskin."

I didn't have a lot of opportunities to play in my backyard with my dad growing up. He worked a lot. He was also diagnosed with rheumatoid arthritis at a very young age, which was really hard on his body. I do remember brief moments though when we did get to play. One day, my cousin and I were in the backyard playing football. My dad joined us. We would punt to him and try and tag him out. We could never catch him. He would punt to us, tag us out, and the next thing you know, it was 4th down. We would punt, couldn't catch him, touchdown! He kicked our butts. We didn't care. He was outside playing with us. Later when I was in junior high, there were a lot more opportunities when he installed a basketball hoop in our driveway. I was getting older, more competitive, and my dad was a competitive man. It stopped being fun when I would get stuffed *every time* I tried a layup. I remember throwing a fit to the point that my dad stopped playing with me. All I have is my regret now.

The first time I watched "Big," all I thought about was how awesome it would be to have that happen so I could give my dad a dose of his own "stuffing" medicine. It was very short-sighted of me, but when you're a kid, you're in the "selfish" moment a lot.

Watching Tom Hanks as an adult child is a treasure you can't forget about. I can only imagine the pure fun that already, "very pleasant" actor had making that movie.

This is the type of movie in which you have to buy the

premise. A boy doesn't want to be a boy anymore, he makes a wish at a coin dispensary machine...that he realizes was unplugged the entire time...

cue chills

...and he wakes up in the morning as Tom Hanks...could've been worse, like Steve Guttenberg or something...

Life as an adult at first is not all that great...gets chased out of his house by his mother, his best friend almost cuts him in half with a hockey stick, he doesn't have anywhere to live or a job.

New meaning to "growing up over night."

This is a Hollywood movie however and he makes it work, almost to the point where he doesn't want to be a boy again, of course, because he falls in love with Elizabeth Perkins.

Who'd wanna go back to acne and awkward junior high dances? Answer: NO-FREAKING-BODY!!!

Like all great movies, there are a lot of great "moments" that everyone refers to: his first encounter with himself in the mirror in the bathroom, his mother chasing him out of the house, the large piano, his "sleep over," and the unplugging of the "Zoltar."

Watching Hanks embrace his inner 12 year old is a lot of fun. When I was a kid, I liked seeing an adult let loose and be goofy like me.

* * *

Adults have a fun time watching him learn about the adult world through a 12 year old's eyes...
...and I feel they learn a little about themselves too.

"This is the woman who I couldn't live with as a husband, and now I'm going to be her son."

I like to call this one "Big-Lite" even if that is a little mean.

A family movie that my parents watched when they were younger and then my siblings and I watched when we were kids was the original "Freaky Friday" with Barbara Harris and a very young Jodie Foster. This was the original. Had this concept been made before this one, I haven't heard about it and don't care to. This premise has spawned at least a dozen more other films of the like, including the recent (and terrible) "The Change-Up."

I feel that "Vice Versa" surpasses "Freaky Friday" in the overall entertainment department.

Judge Reinhold is one of the most enjoyable comedic actors I watched growing up. No one I know can make the large and hilarious facial expressions that he can-- without saying a word--and make people laugh-out-loud like he could. I loved him in both "Beverly Hills Cop" movies (I know there was a third one, I don't count it), "Ruthless People" was good when he was on screen, and his guest appearance on "Seinfeld" as the boyfriend of Elaine who was obsessed with being with Jerry's parents was one-of-a-kind (he received an Emmy nomination).

"Vice Versa" is Reinhold at his best. I feel that "the sell" for movies like this, is having the actors create such distinct characteristics when they are in "their own skin" that when you see them portray their counter-part...it is believable. I feel that Reinhold and Fred Savage did a great job communicating off screen about their approaches--and it shows very well on screen.

Reinhold has a child-like joy in his eye at each moment after the "change" and he never waivers from it. Savage needs to be given credit as well for creating an "adult" child that reminds me of Spok in a way. This comes out in a scene where he is being bullied by kids at school and tries to use "logic" as a shield. It doesn't work out.

I have many favorite scenes in this film, most of them involving Reinhold. I think my favorite is when Reinhold gets his revenge on the bullies at school. It's not what you might expect, but the punishment exceeds their past crimes and gives us a great laugh. Watching his elation in the hallway after doling out their penance is electric and those of us that were bullied (everyone) wishes they could do the same.

At the end of the day, this is a family movie for all ages and a father and son learn how to truly respect and enjoy each other on this journey that they take together.

I don't know anything about Judge Reinhold the person. We always hear stories about Tom Hanks and how wonderful a person he is and that he is friendly. I want to believe the same about Judge Reinhold. In the interviews that I have seen, and the film choices that he has made, he seems like a person that would have a lot of great stories to tell on "game nights" with a cold beer in his hand. I want to keep that impression of him in my mind and "Vice Versa" has a lot to do with that.

Who knows, maybe one day we'll be able to play horseshoes, and he can tell us about being noticed by some fans in the airport as the guy who was "jerking off."

"Look, stars! Ready when you are, Raoul."

The amount of layers with which this next film is brilliant on is what makes it a marvel.

We say that movies are "fun for *ALL* ages" quite often. I honestly believe there is no better truth or way to describe this next film. It has everything: excellent dialogue, a well crafted plot, suspense, great acting, wonderful set pieces, and cartoons...?

Yes, "Who Framed Roger Rabbit" might be one of the most daring projects ever undertaken by a film company.

Now, before I go off on how amazing this movie is, I have a confession to make. At the time of its release in '88, I was in emotional movie limbo. I was turning eleven and I was starting to be influenced by friends at school who were "too cool" for cartoons. I also regrettably did not know who the late great [Bob Hoskins](#) was at the time and was not excited to see the film with him in all of the trailers. Well, I knew who he was after this movie and I appreciated this movie for what it was about 10 years later.

It is a masterpiece.

We have a gumshoe plot set in a world where "Toons" (Bugs Bunny, Mickey Mouse, Donald Duck, and Daffy Duck, etc.) live in our world and are actors and performers just like any other in Hollywood. They reside in Toon Town and interact with live action people all throughout Los Angeles. This premise alone is quite an undertaking, but to have the writers Jeffrey Price and Peter S. Seaman get the dialogue tone and the plotting as perfect as they got it is another layer of remarkable. Add in the acting of Hoskins and Christopher Lloyd (the two live action people that engage with the "Toons" the most) and you have almost everything you need as a director. Robert Zemeckis had his hands full on this picture, but he wasn't unfamiliar with big budget films ("Romancing the Stone" and "Back to the Future" just to name a few of his smaller big budgets...*wink, wink*).

I feel that there was also a part of my subconscious that wanted to hate this movie because Zemeckis delayed the completion and release of the "Back to the Future" sequels in order to complete this project. In retrospect, brilliant move. The eleven-year-old me did not think so.

The "props" department for this film also should be given accolades for adding to the performances by Hoskins and Lloyd. They created 3-D objects that responded to the action the way the cartoons were supposed to on the page. For example, Hoskins wore a spring-loaded metal object shaped like a rabbit that popped out of his shirt on cue like Roger was supposed to in the scene where he hides him under his trench coat. They would later add the animation over the props in post production on Hoskins best take.

Spectacle aside, you have to tell a decent story to be remembered. I feel that they did an excellent job. There are murder mystery elements, characters that return from someone's haunted past, and multiple reveals that are hard to see coming but make sense after we add it all up.

Oh, I forgot to mention Jessica Rabbit...failure on my part. She is voiced by none other than Kathleen Turner. You all know my infatuation with this woman at this point if you have read previous chapters...not gonna lie to you, this movie helped that along.

In the end, a lot of this movie will be remembered for its animated visuals paired very well with its live action counterparts. That is great, but this is also a movie with a lot of originality, intrigue, suspense, and above all, heart.

Where else could you see a taxi cab character open the door of a real car, get into the driver's seat, and drive the car?

"I can't lie to you about your chances, but... you have my sympathies."

I have to do a "two-for" every now and then. These are definitely worthy.

The evolution of this story, like so many others, started with my mother. I remember her always referring to the first movie in the series as the "scariest movie" she'd ever seen. She mentioned it in passing when I was about 5 and I never forgot it. I was not allowed to watch it at that time given my age.

Approximately 6 years later, the sequel was the Sunday Night movie on ABC (I think--one of the big four networks, anyway). My father was very excited when he found out and started queuing up a tape. I remember the ominous score at the beginning as a very small spacecraft was docked onto a larger one. The speed with which the engineers cut through the metal doors is an image I will probably never forget.

This was my first exposure to what would be the greatest hero I have ever seen captured on film.

I both loved and hated Sunday Night movies. It gave me plenty of opportunities to be exposed to a number of different movies and it was edited for television, so my parents generally always let me watch them. I still had an 8 o'clock bed time and that meant I never got to finish the movies unless we recorded them. I got an hour at most (more like 40 minutes of real time due to the commercials) and I always slept poorly on those nights because I wanted to know what was going to happen next. I remember being able to vaguely hear some of the louder action scenes from where I laid in my bed that night.

The last scene I remember before having to go to bed is when Bishop did the famous "knife trick" over Hudson's hand. There was much that I was already confused about, like when Ripley discovers that Bishop is an android and she loses her shit on him and the rest of the command crew, why she was having nightmares, etc.

The next day, I decided rather than finish this movie, I'd rather watch the original. I was already getting my arguments ready for my mom in my head right before I asked her. I didn't need them.

"You're old enough now," she said. "You have to watch it with me and your father though."

Deal!

My mom was not lying. "Alien" was a creepy trip.

The quiet, anxiety tone that they create builds the perfect tension for later "jump" scenes. The concept of a "birth" occurring and unleashing one of the greatest murdering-machine villains of all time is beyond creative. It was unlike anything I had ever heard of.

My mom told me after we watched it why it was so scary for her the first time around. My dad took her to this movie blind. She knew nothing about it, had not seen any previews, and did not know what to expect. She was not mentally ready for what she was going to view.

Luckily, she was kind enough to give me 6 years to mentally prepare for my first viewing.

I mentioned that Ripley is the greatest hero captured on film. That wasn't bullshit, or an overstatement. She is my favorite hero to watch to this day. She is smart, calm under pressure, inventive, and does not like to take any chances (listening to her discuss their options with the rest of the crew is one of the best bits of acting and dialogue in this well written feature). She is willing to do everything necessary to keep herself and her crew alive. Unfortunately, her foe is just as crafty, and about 100 times stronger in a physical contest. Watching Ellen Ripley develop from a "background" character into the leader and survivor that she becomes is a joy.

The sequel, "AlienS," is a very appropriate title. Our heroes, a crew of marines, go to the planet that Ripley and her original crew found the first alien on. The planet is now inhabitable and has a small town of people mining the resources there...that is, they thought they were and have now lost contact with them. Ripley is eventually convinced to go and tries to warn everyone as to how things are more likely to go poorly before they get better. The prideful female marine, Vasquez, interrupts her warning and arrogantly lets her know that if Ripley shows her where they are, she will take care of the rest. Ripley wants to believe her, but we can see and hear it in her voice that she doesn't.

* * *

Remember how I said "AlienS" was an appropriate title. They didn't bring enough bullets. Their first encounter is a disaster and more than half their company is wiped out. Maybe three aliens get killed in the process, one of them by Ripley when she takes charge and drives their RV into where the retreating marines are, to extract them. Whatever confidence the marines had is now lost and people start to take Ripley seriously.

I love both of these films for very different reasons. "Alien" is an imaginative horror story all about mood and tone and begs us to ask "what is going to happen next?"

"Aliens" is a very well written and acted action extravaganza with amazing set pieces, props, special effects, camera tricks, and a well developed multi-dimensional calm and collected Ellen Ripley.

"Aliens" also has one of the best [action scores ever written](). I made mention of [James Horner]() when I wrote about "Krull" and listed "Aliens" among the best of his work. It holds up today and ad agencies still use it in their trailers.

For those of you that have not taken the time to watch these, prepare yourselves. Dedicate some time and watch them back-to-back, preferably with someone that has already seen them and loves them.

Is there a greater way to watch a movie new to you?

"You know, if everyone is as nice as you, country hospitality is gonna get an awful name."

In the late 80s early 90s, my dad and I started filling out March Madness Brackets and entering them into a pool where he worked at the local brotherhood of electricians bureau.

He and I never won, but we had fun filling the bracket out, talking strategy, and picking the underdogs we wanted to win.

From an NBA perspective, I remember watching the L. A. Lakers and the Boston Celtics playing in the finals throughout the 80s.

Sports was another thing that my father and I enjoyed doing together. I don't think he missed more than a handful of my soccer games my entire life, including college.

The same joy a father has watching his sons play or a son having his dad there at a game, is the kind of joy that exudes from every pore of [David Anspaugh](#)'s "Hoosiers."

There are a lot of great "sports" movies. "Bull Durham," "[The Natural](#)," "[Rudy](#)" (also by Anspaugh), "[The Longest Yard](#)," etc. "Hoosiers" stands well above the rest of them. I remember us (my dad, mom, me, and my little brother) watching it two days in a row when we rented it.

That's not something that we did together consistently unless ALL of us were really excited about a movie. "Hoosiers" was one of those movies.

The "based on a true story" element is what makes this movie so great. If this were a made-up Hollywood script, we'd be annoyed with the cliche ending. There is something about the underdog story that compels me to excitement, and when it can happen for real, well that just gives everyone in America hope.

We start off with a gruff coach in a small town. The town does not want to embrace his philosophy for the local High School Basketball team.

I have talked about Alec Guinness quite possibly being my favorite actor of all time. Gene Hackman is 1B.

I can't think of a line that he has delivered on film that I didn't feel he believed as the character he portrayed. His subtleties with voice inflection and expression give us a lot of communication--while still being very small on the screen. Making that look easy is why actors like Guinness and Hackman become film legends. If anyone has seen themselves on tv, be it a home video or the like, it is very easy to tell how "big" your expressions become when the camera is rolling. The camera doesn't miss a lot. Hackman is very controlled, even when the script requires him shouting to his team from the sideline, or when he needs to coach a kid on the bench.

I know that I have not talked about the movie that much. I am doing that on purpose. For those of you that are my consistent readers and have not seen it yet, I'd jump "Hoosiers" to the top of your list. There are great performances from Hackman (as always), Dennis Hopper (who got himself an Oscar nomination for that role), and Barbara Hershey (a woman that I feel is very underrated in terms of the roles she has portrayed on screen--check out her filmography. She's really good--a favorite of mine is "The Stunt Man").

I dare you not to have an emotional reaction to the ending of this film.

"JUST a bit outside."

The only thing I think I like more than a movie with heart, is a movie that tricks me into believing it is just another screwball comedy; but then it develops into a film with a decent amount of heart.

That is precisely what this next feature did to me in my experience with it.

I know, two sports movies in a row, but they are completely different.

"Hoosiers" is a flat out well crafted high school basketball drama. "Major League" is about baseball, and does have a lot of screwball comedy elements, but it uplifts us in the end unexpectedly.

I loved watching comedies with my dad. He didn't laugh a lot. When we had a movie that could get him to chuckle, we all enjoyed it. He had a great laugh. It might have been great to all of us because it was so infrequent. I just remember loving the sound of it. This movie made my dad laugh-out-loud frequently.

Like most comedies, the premise is quite simple. The owner of the Cleveland Indians wants to move the team to a more pleasant city. Her plan, fire all of the best players and managers and hire a group of "has-beens" and green "up-and-comers" so that she can pay them less money, they'll stink, no one will come to the games--thus, it will be easier to move the team. The General Manager doesn't like the sound of that and helps put together a team that looks like the one the owner is trying for, but really has the ability to be great if they can pull it all together.

And we're off.

The cast is amazing. Tom Berenger is the lead "has-been" catcher, who is tasked with helping Ricky "Wild Thing" Vaughn (Charlie Sheen in an underrated performance) get his rocket arm under control.

My family and I for the most part love Tom Berenger. I call him "Rutger Hauer" lite. I especially like him in comedic roles, but he has the presence to be haunting as well like he was in "Platoon." I have to plug one of his lesser known films here, "The Last of the Dogmen," he's great in it along with Barbara Hershey, again. Great story. Go see it.

Along with Berenger and Sheen we have Corbin Bernsen as an overpaid "has-been" that is not playing as hard as he should be. There is also Wesley Snipes as Willie Mays Hayes, the best named character in the movie, he's a young up-and-comer that is as fast as Rickey Henderson.

My favorite casting in this movie, however, is the gruff James Gammon as the man hired to manage the team.

Gammon is one of those actors that you are familiar with because he gets a lot of different roles in a lot of different kinds of movies, but he is never a lead. This is the movie I will always remember him for. His reluctance to take the job when he is first approached by the GM is one of the first laugh-out-loud moments that my father and I shared. Well written and acted.

Add in Rene Russo, veteran Chelcie Ross, and a very young and buff Dennis Haysbert and you have a mostly undiscovered cast of future talent ready to explode onto the screen.

The written quote I listed for the title of this chapter doesn't give it justice. The delivery by my favorite play caller of all time, Bob Uecker, makes it one of the funniest situations and lines in the film. I get excited for every scene in which he gets to make a call in this movie, and his comedic timing is priceless.

Comedies are the most impressionable movies on children. You learn so much from them. There are elements of comedy that are precise, calculated, and well executed; and sometimes, a baseball hits someone in the balls and we laugh. This movie has all of these elements and doesn't come off as too heavy on either end of the spectrum.

Back to the heart.

This is a movie that forces you to laugh given the comedic situations that the writer has created, but the climax of the film gives me goosebumps. Every decision that writer/director David S. Ward created for the "big game" was done as well as any sports drama and to be surprised with the "plan" and not the outcome is a pure joy to experience and watch, not only for the first time, but again and again.

* * *

This is a movie my dad and I used to catch on television when we were flipping through the channels. It always caused pause.

"Let's get to the rat kill'n'."

I was having a discussion with an author colleague about how I wanted to do a post on my favorite John Wayne movies growing up. He said it'd be a good idea so I'm doing it.

We'll see how this goes...I'd like to start off with some impressionable JW films and then I'll leave my favorite of all time for last. "The Cowboys" is on this list somewhere in the middle.

"The Man Who Shot Liberty Vallance" had one of the best cast compilations of its time. Jimmy Stewart, John Wayne, Lee Marvin, Vera Miles, and of course John Ford directed. Valance, played by the haunting Lee Marvin, is a bully of a man that terrorizes everyone in the valley. Jimmy Stewart as Ransom Stoddard is the local would be politician that would stand up to Valance, because he doesn't know any better. John Wayne as Tom Doniphon is the "man's man" (of course) that is there to help Stoddard along the way as Doniphon is the only man that Valance would not dare cross. Would you? It is a well told story with old western politics as the back drop for a movie about bullying and standing up for what's right. Great performances all around.

"The Searchers" is a very interesting performance by Wayne. He is such a hater as Ethan Edwards in this movie that it is hard to like him, even if you think his hate stems from the "just" side of things. This movie is daunting, ensnaring, and suspenseful, right up to the climax. I'd like not to give anything away, other than Edwards is a man searching--for what feels like a lifetime--for his niece that has been taken by a Comanche tribe. That is not all he is searching for, but saying too much about that would ruin your first viewing and I won't get into the metaphors here. A must see for film buffs.

"El Dorado" is just a fun movie. Along Wayne it stars Robert Mitchum (one of his real life drinking buddies), and a very young James Caan. There is a story about water and land rights that gets in the way of the chemistry of Wayne, Mitchum, and Caan. The scenes they share together are electric and I wish they had more. It's an entertaining Western with high comedy, action, gun fights and horse chases.

"Rio Bravo" is another entertaining Wayne film, but it is not just about the humor. Though there is plenty humor, there is tension, drama, suspense, action, and of course, gun fights. Get a load of this cast: Dean Martin, Ricky Nelson, Angie Dickinson, and Walter Brennan to name a few that you will remember. Quentin Tarantino has been quoted mentioning this as one of his top five favorite films of all time, along with "The Good, the Bad, and the Ugly." I would say it is a favorite Wayne film, but it is also one of the greatest Westerns ever made. Check it out.

"McLintock!" fits the mold of a romantic comedy that happens to be set in the old west. That is one of the great things about it. You won't find any gunfights here. Just some very well written humor of all types including sarcasm, sass, and slapstick; all of which Wayne and

Maureen O'Hara find themselves at home in, as a couple that is struggling to make their complicated marriage work. There are some great supporting performances by Chill Wills as Drago and Patrick Wayne--John Wayne's real life son who plays the love interest of McLintock's (Wayne's) daughter Becky in the movie. A mouthful I know. Campy comedy. Go see it.

"Red River" is probably the most well crafted Western that I have ever seen. It centers around a cattle drive by a baron, Thomas Dunson (played by Wayne in his best acting performance that I can recall), who is a ruthless man. During the drive, Wayne becomes so cruel that his adopted son Matt (Montgomery Clift) revolts and leaves him on his own out in the wilderness. The cattle men on the drive are more than happy to follow Matt. The movie takes a turn here and we follow both story lines as they are set for impact at the film's climax. Hands down the feature that should be rented first for film buffs. Don't hesitate.

"Bullshit. What's the Job?"-"I love it when you talk dirty."

I mentioned in an earlier chapter that "The Naked Gun" was probably my first exposure to a true farce. That was false.

I'm still surprised how early I was allowed to see "Blazing Saddles."

So, one weekend every summer, my mom went off to a woman's retreat, leaving us home alone with dad. We lived on eggs, cereal, hot dogs, and Ramen Noodles.

Yep.

Now, dad was a little more lenient than mom when it came to TV and movie viewership. We (me and my big sister and little brother) knew that. Did we take advantage?

Hell yes.

A few weeks prior to my mom leaving for her retreat, I remembered walking through the living room and observing my parents laughing at what they were watching, until they noticed me.

Mom: "This isn't for you to see."

Me: "What is it?"

Dad: "A Funny movie."

* * *

Mom: "It's for adults."

Me: "What's the name of it?"

Dad: "Blazing Saddles."

Game over. I had a title. I knew mom was leaving. It was a matter of time before I talked my dad into letting me watch it. It wasn't hard.

Me: "Dad, can we watch 'Blazing Saddles' with you?"

Dad: "Sure....don't tell your mother."

Did I get all of the jokes? Hell no. But I had a dad that was more than happy to explain them to me.

I always thought my dad was an impatient man, and he was about certain things. He was very impatient with my ability to complete chores. That was my major interaction with my dad, so I, of course, always felt that he was an impatient, short tempered man. Looking back, there are plenty of moments where he displayed patience regularly. Watching movies with the kids is one of them.

Me: "Dad? What's a shit-kicker?"

Dad: (giggles) "It's a mean name for a cowboy."

Me: "Oh."

That was most of the movie. Luckily dad had seen it

enough to humor us throughout the viewing. Listening to my dad laugh along with us was like hearing The Beatles for the first time. It was something new and wonderful and you didn't want the song to end on the radio. I have mentioned before that my dad was not one for laughter often. A trait that I have inherited from him. Watching "Blazing Saddles" with him was like listening to 5 of The Beatles greatest hits in a row on the radio.

My dad loved the ability to "pause" tapes. He grew up without a VCR and never had a chance to "stop" the things he was viewing. It seemed like we were giving him a chance to control the world when we had a question and he could grab the remote, click "pause," and explain a scene to us. He enjoyed it, and he was good at it. This happened every time we watched some dialogue we didn't understand and dad had a huge laugh.

I remember laughing at the funny faces, sounds, and slapstick of Blazing Saddles when I was younger. Viewing it as I grew, I started laughing at the scenes my dad laughed at.

What an amazing movie. The courage to take on a film like this deserves accolades itself. No way could this movie be made in this day and age of political correctness. Is that a good thing? Probably. Am I thankful this movie got made? Yeppers.

[Mel Brooks](#) to me, is the godfather of Farcical Comedy, without a lot of competition. He makes films that can make a child laugh for the reasons I mentioned above and have the wit to keep an adult's attention with clever writing, and satire that strikes true. That is not an easy thing to do and he will never get the artistic credit that he deserves. It's a shame that comedies--aren't taken more seriously????

What the hell do I know?

I know three things in retrospect watching "Blazing Saddles" over 5 times over the years: 1) Richard Pryor is one of the greatest comedic writers of all time 2) Adults enjoy the layers of wit that occurs in the dialogue of EVERY Mel Brooks movie 3) Campfire farting scenes will always make any person laugh-out-loud.

Basically, the film is about a greedy railroad entrepreneur that cannot get a town to yield their land. They try to strong arm them, but that does not work. They send in a black sheriff to help them, with the idea that it will cause internal strife so that they will destroy themselves from the inside out. Shenanigans ensue on many, many, many, different levels--including breaking the "5th wall," in which they fight into another Hollywood set of a musical production.

The cast is amazing:

Cleavon Little,

Gene Wilder,

the underrated and amazing Harvey Korman,

Slim Pickens,

* * *

Madeline Kahn,

and a short/hilarious performance by Dom Deluise.

Reading through the quotes to pick one for this post was a mild joy. I laughed reading them, visualizing the scenes again in my head. Rarely can a movie do that and it's pure exuberance when that can happen.

What people need to understand before they watch this movie is that it is a total satire-farce on every level and is never supposed to be taken seriously. This is not a film for the easily offended, but for the person that can think about what the writers are trying to say between the lines...and snicker with them.

"Why's he calling me meat? I'm the one driving a Porsche."

Prior to watching "Bull Durham," my experience with baseball in movies was "The Natural," and "Major League." Two very different movies.

"The Natural" was all about the passion and drama that comes with the love of baseball. Upping the stakes, at a big game to win it all. Pitching, home runs, the high-light reel, etc.

"Major League" starts off as a screwball and ends up having a shining moment as epic as any baseball scene in sports movies, over the ages.

"Bull Durham," was somewhere in between the two and was more about taking the glamour out of the game and writing a travelogue of how hard the minor-league life is. It is a very well written story centered around a woman who fancies herself as a baseball "theologian."

Annie Savoy (played by a very sexy Susan Sarandon--in this role any way) is a woman that takes it upon herself to "date" one member of the local Durham Bull's baseball club a year. She brags that this generally gets them to "The Show," thus only allowing her one relationship per season.

Her two candidates are Ebby Calvin "Nuke" LaLoosh (played brilliantly by a very young and energetic Tim Robbins) and the wily veteran, Crash Davis (Kevin Costner).

* * *

Crash diplomatically relieves himself from the competition with a very poetic monologue, and Annie realizes that her approach was a huge mistake.

Crash and Annie both take on Nuke as a men-tee, with very different tactics, obviously. Annie is a nurturer/lover and educates him with poetry, spirituality, and "magic" garments...?

Crash is a tough love father figure. Crash's nickname for Ebby is way more fitting than "Nuke," IMO...he even goes so far as to tell the opposing hitter what the pitch will be when Ebby "shakes" Crash off.

I remember this as the first movie I had seen referring to the majors as, "The Show." I love that.

The film consists of many well written scenes. The dialogue is original and witty. It's safe to say that writer/director Ron Shelton has spent some time traveling from town-to-town on a few minor league buses.

That is the essence of the movie. The experience of being on a minor league team.

It is very quotable:

Skip: You guys. You lollygag the ball around the infield. You lollygag your way down to first. You lollygag in and out of the dugout. You know what that makes you? Larry!

Larry: Lollygaggers!

* * *

Skip: Lollygaggers. What's our record, Larry?

Larry: Eight and sixteen.

Skip: Eight... and sixteen. How'd we ever win eight?

Larry: It's a miracle.

Skip: It's a miracle. This... is a simple game. You throw the ball. You hit the ball. You catch the ball.

This scene is of course delivered by the late great Trey Wilson (mentioned in "Raising Arizona") as Skip and Robert Wuhl as Larry. I feel it is one of the great moments in movies about sports. There is purpose to it for all of the characters involved, and at the end of the day, you get a great laugh. Did I mention that Skip decided to deliver this message when they were all in the shower room after having grabbed a pile of baseball bats--and in dramatic fashion--throwing them at their feet?

Even though there is a lacking in the glamour of baseball in this picture, Ron Shelton treats baseball with the utmost respect. The title character has made a religion from baseball, and Crash cannot help himself from causing humiliation and harm to Nuke when he feels he "disrespects" the game.

Don't expect any game winning home runs, or bases loaded strike outs, but this movie bleeds baseball in every bit of dialogue from three very passionate players.

* * *

Just remember: "The rose goes in front, big guy."

Words to live by...

"What happened to Sully?" -- "I let him go."

I have only one thing to be thankful to for this next chapter—ABC's "Sunday Night Movies."

For those of you that don't know what that means, back before we had all the technologies that we have now (DVDs, BlueRays, Streaming, OnDemand, etc.) and prior to VCRs being *too* popular, movies used to have a much longer "window" of time prior to being released on VHS. Once they were released on VHS, the rental stores rarely had enough copies for a very popular new release (they'd usually have about 5 copies for a *very* popular movie) to go around if you really wanted to see a movie. I found that by the time you could finally get a copy of the new release you wanted to see, you would've already seen it on ABC's "Sunday Night Movies"--however, it was edited for television....why else would my parents let me see it?

Ok, confession time again... "The Terminator" was not the first "Schwarzenegger movie" that I ever saw. It was "Commando" on "Sunday Night!"

Is this movie a "classic" or "must see" per say?

Hell no!

Am I glad I got to see it?

Yes.

* * *

It introduced me to Schwarzenegger, in which he became a sub-genre of Action movies in-and-of-himself. I always heard my friends at school that were allowed to watch his movies (unedited) talking about how "awesome" they were. After I watched "Commando," I completely understood what they were talking about.

Action! Action! Action!

I think by today's standards, the movie might drag in parts...but at the time, it was an extravaganza.

His daughter's kidnap and chase down his mountain fortress, his free-fall from the bowels of the airplane, the pursuit of Sully through the mall, the battle with Cooke at the Motel, the extraction of all of the weapons at the sporting goods store, and the final sequence when he attempts to rescue his daughter are some of the action set pieces in the film.

I also found that in his movies, he took notes from James Bond and started having cool witty phrases after he murdered a villain. The "catch phrases" are considered cliche now, because of Bond and Schwarzenegger.

The movie has a very simple premise: John's (Schwarzenegger's) daughter is kidnapped as collateral by some mercenaries that want John Matrix (how cool is that name) to assassinate a political figure in a far off country overseas. The flight overseas is 14 hours. That is all the time he has to track the villains, find out his daughter's location, get to her, and attempt her rescue.

* * *

BOOM!

I found that making light of the murders with his catch phrases made the movie less gruesome. After all, they were villains and we wanted him to kill them (come on, they kidnapped his daughter). I also enjoyed the performance of [Rae Dawn Chong](#).

She plays Cindy, an innocent woman that is at first hijacked by John Matrix and forced to do some unpleasant things for him. She is reluctant to help John Matrix (I just love that damn name) at first for good reason, but is eventually won over and becomes his ally.

I liked her anxious flare and watching her arm and discharge a rocket launcher is priceless.

Again, this is a movie that helped create the "cliche action" movies that we make light of and laugh with now. If it was not for movies like this and the Stallone "Rambo" series, we wouldn't have the pleasure of enjoying movies like "Hot Shots" I and II. Which I found pleasure in watching, very much.

"Gradual school is where you go to school and you gradually find out you don't want to go to school anymore."

My conservative family (mom and dad) are very interesting to me.

They knew that when they first saw this next film, they were watching excellence, even though a lot of the source material made them feel uncomfortable.

To me, it is truly a masterpiece, and one of the most well written and clever films I've seen.

Given that the material is drawn from a John Irving novel would probably make it seem pretty easy to create a masterpiece script, however, "Cider House Rules" was also adapted from a JI novel...and that was a POS...IMO.

This film is not a POS. It is an energetic yet smooth, strange gem, with actors that fit the roles they are given perfectly. I cannot imagine anyone else being portrayed by another actor, even down to James McCall, who had the difficult task of depicting our young protagonist.

"The World According to Garp" is one of the best screenplays out there. Steve Tesich deserves accolades for adapting a decent novel into a perfect screenplay.

Robin Williams is superb as T. S. Garp. Watching him

for the first time, I found I was wondering why he had so much restraint. After about five minutes into his performance, I remembered thinking, o*h, Robin wants to be an actor in this, not a comedian*...man could he deliver when he needed to.

[Glenn Close](#) as Garp's mother Jenny Fields is so....interesting. She is interesting because she finds EVERYTHING interesting.

She encourages her son in everything that he does, and doesn't bat an eye when he wants to be a writer. The irony comes when she decides to be a writer and is able to generate a book that outsells all of his combined and then some. The underlying annoyance that Garp holds for his mother's success as a writer is one of the subtle maneuvers that makes his performance sparkle. He is happy for her and the success she has, while he is annoyed that she can somehow steal his thunder in his profession. She's a nurse dammit! So real.

[John Lithgow](#) as Roberta Muldoon, an ex Philadelphia Eagle tight end, is a performance for the ages. His ability to depict a man that has decided he is a woman, and not make it foolish to the point that we laugh "at" instead of "with" is a feat all its own.

Outside of maybe [Walter Brennan](#), is there a better supporting/character actor out there other than John Lithgow? What can't he play? He was easily cast against "type" in this role, and he tackled it with ferocious abandon. Show me any other man that is over 6 feet tall in Hollywood that could portray Roberta with such humanity....

* * *

.....

Yeah, I thought so.

Talking about him prior to having seen it, you would most likely believe it wouldn't work on film. I'm here to tell you it not only works, it's not even a distraction-- slightly. He doesn't overplay it, he doesn't undersell it-- it's a perfect mix at baseline and it's a captivating experience when you see it.

Trying to explain the story would not be fair to anyone interested in watching this movie. It is simply the "The World According to Garp" and you need to experience his point of view for the first time fresh.

I will say that George Roy Hill was a genius for deciding to bookend this movie with "When I'm 64" by the Beatles. He had me at "When I get older, losing my hair..."

I plug every movie I write about.

Move this one to the top of the list.

It'll deliver.

"Hi. How're you doing? I'm the Easter Bunny."

Oh man, this one is going to be another tough one, I can feel it.

I was just reading through some of the quotes and my eyes started tearing up reading them and thinking about my first viewing. What an experience.

Movie night with my parents as a kid was like a surprise birthday party. I was young and involved in sports so I didn't watch a lot of television and didn't see a lot of trailers. Plus, if the TV was on, I was playing The Legend of Zelda on my Nintendo Entertainment System. I didn't care how many times I beat it, I kept playing that damn game over and over again.

Anyways....

I'd come home from a practice and I'd see some rentals in their clear plastic cases on the counter.

They would always rent a "new release" and an "old" movie that they wanted to share with us. This experience was a "new release" and it was one of the most emotional experiences that I have had with a film on its first viewing.

Before I say anything else, I want to share that I am not a baseball "fan" per say. I can sit and watch a game with my friends given the perfect set of circumstances. I understand the game enough to know the strategy and the lingo, but I'd rather watch football, basketball or soccer.

With that said, there is nothing like going to the ball park, getting a dog and a beer and relaxing in the sun.

Even if you are not a baseball fan, this movie can help you appreciate why people are still so enthusiastic about experiencing it.

"Field of Dreams" is about why there is passion for baseball. It has moments where I watch it and think that W.P. Kinsella (novel) and Phil Alden Robinson (screenplay) conspired to answer an elementary short essay, "Why do you love baseball?"

Watching James Earl Jones as Terence Mann and Burt Lancaster as Archibald "Moonlight" Graham as they monologue on their different reasons for loving the sport is more than inspiring. I can get goosebumps thinking about their descriptions. Lets be honest, listening to James Earl Jones read the back of a cereal box can give you goosebumps.

All of that is great, but the heart of the movie comes from Ray Kinsella (Kevin Costner). We learn very early on that his father, John, was also a man that had a passion for baseball like Terence and Archibald. Throughout the film it is learned that Ray's rebellion with his father happened at a young age when he rejected the sport that his father loved so much. Ray remembers feeling wrong for having rebelled against baseball and his father and always felt that there was a necessary apology that he was never able to make before his father passed.

This of course is told appropriately over the course of the film and delivered in a most well written fashion.
I remember enjoying the energy that Annie Kinsella (Amy Madigan) displayed in her effort to support the eccentric decisions that her husband decides to make throughout the movie, along with influencing their daughter and community to make healthy decisions. When she is able to inspire people in their town to choose not to ban a book at their local schools, it is both humorous and moving.

[Ray Liotta](#) as Shoeless Joe Jackson is played with the correct level of poise and passion for such an iconic Major League figure. When he talks about putting a glove to his nose with his bright blue eyes, he almost looks hypnotized. I wanted to go grab my glove and smell it while he was talking about it (I didn't need to, I could smell the glove where I was sitting...I think I was hypnotized).

This is the first film I recall watching where my dad could not contain the tears. They poured from him at the film's climax after Terence disappears into the corn and Ray Kinsella demands clarity from Shoeless Joe.
I found later that my dad's father had a very similar story to John Kinsella. He played in the minors and was on the cusp of moving up into the majors, but made some choices in his life that impeded this.

Like Ray Kinsella giving out hints about his relationship with his father throughout the movie, my dad gave me as many clues about his relationship with his father throughout his life with me. This is the movie that got my dad talking with me about his baseball experiences...and sometimes, when I was lucky, a little more.

"Walter? Walter? Walter!"

Whoever coined the phrase, you always remember your first(s), was not lying.

My first kiss--Beth Eddington. I was six. We obviously didn't know what we were doing and we closed our eyes too soon and bonked each other with our noses. Our lips touched. Hers were wet, mine were dry...
...

...that was about it. I ran away, blushing. She smiled and watched me act like my hair was on fire.

I remember the first time I scored a goal playing soccer. It was my third year playing. We had a pretty decent team and a great coach. I was in the box, there was a square pass made to me and I kicked it as hard as I could at the net, past the goalie. I was pretty close, it wasn't very fair. After I got my first one, they just started flooding in and I can't remember any of the rest.

Just like after your first goal when there are many more goals to quickly follow, such was the case with the first Cary Grant movie that I ever watched. I had to watch many more.

I've discussed a lot of the bonding that I'd done with my dad and movies on this blog. Time to share about my mom too. We absolutely loved Cary Grant, and "Father Goose" was a pure joy to watch. When Cary Grant passed, one of the networks (I can't remember which one) ran a late evening marathon over the weekend of a lot of Grant's pictures. We discovered the marathon right before "Father Goose" started and my mom grabbed a tape and we started recording. Standard practice at this point.

We took turns "pausing out" the commercials.

As I was looking for quotes, there were so many well crafted moments, that it was hard to pick just one. It was a movie that had such well written dialogue delivered by so many talented people, that it is truly an underrated Grant gem. My mom and I weren't the only ones that thought so. Peter Stone, Frank Tarloff, and S.H. Barnett won the Oscar for Best Writing, Story, and Screenplay Written Directly for the Screen in 1965. The Oscars and I rarely agree...an exception I'm glad to concede.

Being that this was my first experience with Cary Grant, a decade later I found out that he was an Englishman (in real life that is) and was dumbfounded. In this and many of the other roles he portrayed in American films...he was an American. He would always, in some way be, the unshaven, un-bathed, crusty old American drunkard, Walter Eckland, who ends up being responsible for the lives of a school teacher and her female students on an isolated island during World War II.

I've raved about Grant, Leslie Caron as, "Catherine Louise Marie Ernestine Freneau," was given a role of a lifetime and did beyond her very best with it. The chemistry that Grant and Caron were able to share in this picture goes right alongside Spencer Tracy and Katharine Hepburn as one of the greatest pairings on film--in my book any way.

It would be a shame not to mention the great Trevor Howard as Commander Frank Houghton. He plays the "friend" responsible for conning Walter into taking a job reporting enemy war craft that he spots while remaining on an isolated island after an unfortunate "accident" with Walter's boat and the Commander's ship. The majority of the dialogue shared between Walter and Houghton is over the radio; cut and edited to perfection by Ted J. Kent.

The comedic timing portrayed between Grant and Caron on the island and with Howard over the radio was not only entertaining, I haven't seen this type of scenario performed better in movies that share the same ploy. The closest is probably the scene in "Roxanne" when C. D. is trying to help Chris woo Roxanne in person while Chris wears a listening device under an Elmer Fudd cap. Again, that is one scene. Grant, Caron, and Howard did it similarly throughout multiple scenes of an entire motion picture.

I know that I have not talked about the scenes in detail. Again, I do that because I do not want to spoil the comedy that you will find viewing this film fresh for the first time.

Enjoy.

"If you can dream it, you can do it."

I watched a TON of Disney movies growing up. I don't just mean their animated movies. We had cable television from 1980-1984. That included the Disney Channel. Not to mention, ABC aired two-and-a-half Disney movies a week after school from 4pm-5pm Mountain Time until I was about 12 years old (1989-it might have gone on longer, but I started competitive sports around that age and watched way less television because of practice after school).

Being that there were so many, a lot of them flow together in my mind ("Bedknobs and Broomsticks," "Mary Poppins," "Chitty Chitty Bang Bang," "The Gnome Mobile," "Pete's Dragon," etc.). All of these are great, but they do not stand out apart in my mind. There are four that do:

"Pollyanna"

I love movies that have heart. This one is huge. I remember watching a bunch of boring, snobby adults at the beginning of this movie. Enter Pollyanna. Hayley Mills as a child star in the 60s for Disney was what Henry Thomas and River Phoenix were as child stars in the 80s. This is the first movie I remember watching where I saw a young lady light up the screen by walking into frame. The costumes, lighting, and direction deserve a lot of that credit, but there was nothing like young Hayley Mills. To watch the story of a very depressed neighborhood being influenced on very deep emotional levels by an unapologetic, inspiring little

Buddha of a girl was quite moving. Like "E. T." this movie made me feel many emotions from beginning to end and I challenge people that generally cry at movies not to cry at this one.

"The Shaggy Dog"

There is a lot of cool stuff about this movie. A boy that gets cursed and turns into a dog. It sounds like a horror movie, and it does have some of those elements, but it plays as a mild-adventure/comedy. It has Annette Funicello (hubba hubba) as the teenage love interest and one of my favorite underrated actors, Fred MacMurray as the father. Its' a very interesting comedy with slight dark elements and a loving boy that wants to protect his family. It stuck with me I think because of the transformation special effects. I saw it at a very young age, before I was jaded and thought that cursed people might really turn into dogs.

"The Parent Trap"

Sweet Hayley again, and this time, it's double trouble. I love the story. Twin sisters, who had no clue about the other, meet at camp for the first time, and decide to switch places (the daughter that lives with mother goes home with dad and vice versa). Needless to say, shenanigans ensue in many different scenes and the story ends up taking off on levels that I didn't see coming. This film features Brian Keith (another underrated actor) and the boisterous Maureen O'Hara. The story and the acting all around are what stuck with me over the years with this romantic comedy, and I try and watch it at least once a year.

...and my favorite Disney "kids" movie (probably of all time)...

"The Absent Minded Professor"

This was a visual extravaganza for me at a very young age. I wanted flubber to be real, so bad. I was a runt of a kid and I could've used anti-gravity on many occasions at recess. To see a man role up flubber into a ball and watch it continue to bounce and bounce all over the room was incredible to me. I couldn't look away. My dad was a racquet ball player and the balls that the professor made reminded me of the racquet balls my dad had lying around the house when he came home from a match. Our unlikely hero used flubber on his shoes at a dance to impress some town folk (and his estranged love interest), on the local height-challenged varsity basketball team's sneakers, and on his own shoes to fight local gangsters. I can't wait to revisit it again, soon.

"Stick around."

Remember when I mentioned that thing about "firsts?" Here's another one. It's a little more "abstract" for a "first," but a type of "first" none-the-less.

So, the first [Arnold Schwarzenegger](#) movie I ever saw was "[Commando](#)," Sunday Night Movie and edited for television. The second was "[The Terminator](#)," also edited for television.

This next one was the first one I was allowed to watch, with my dad, completely unedited on VHS.

It starts like "[The Magnificent Seven](#)," and ends up being "[Silver Bullet](#)."

A special military team is sent into the jungle on what is believed to be a rescue mission. As we start our journey with them, they prove to be a formidable force.

Prior to reaching the enemy outpost, they discover a multitude of concerning circumstances that no one can explain. There was another team that went missing on the same mission. The group stumbles along their aircraft, and can find no explanation as to why it was brought down. They also find a large majority of the team members corpses, hanging from a tree with their hides removed. They know it is them because of their dog tags.

Bent on retribution now, they invade the enemy hideaway with stealth precision and eliminate all of them with no casualties on their team.

Dutch (Schwarzenegger) finds out that it was anything *but* a rescue mission all along and he has been duped by an old "friend." They have also been cut off from their transport out, and have to take "the long way" around the South American Jungle.

Little did any of them know that this would be the least of their problems.

At the very, very start of this movie, there appears to be a "Mothership" alien vessel that launches a life pod down through earth's atmosphere. I always felt that this would've been a slightly more interesting movie if they would've left that scene out of the beginning. Jim & John Thomas developed a great script with disturbing visuals and haunting scenes that created a lot of suspense as we watch our heroes trudge along in the forest, only to get picked off one by one. Being that we as the viewer are in on the "alien invasion," we don't get to be in the thick of it with the heroes as much, knowing that they are being hunted by a monster from another world.

Don't get me wrong, "Predator" is still one bad ass action extravaganza that changed the way I'd play with my G. I. Joe action figures moving forward. I remember looking at all of the action figures I had, and compiling a team much like the one in the movie. I would get all of the similar weapons that they had in the movie and match them up with the character's and pick them off one by one. The problem was, I did not have a predator action figure, so that was all make-believe (i.e. me). I still pretty much reenacted this movie when I played with my G. I. Joe's, predator available or not.

I remember being so thankful that my mom allowed me to watch that movie with my dad. I could finally share in some of the conversations my friends had at school about the movie. It also loosened my parents up a little on future "R" rated movies.

Pretty good "first" ...

...even if it is a little abstract.

"...nothing grinds my gears worse than some chowderhead that doesn't know when to keep his big trap shut..."

This movie was viewed on the down low and never mentioned to my parents.

When you hear the title, you'll laugh at that notion. You have to remember that my parents were 80s conservative in Idaho. That's like America 50s conservative for the rest of the world at that time...and I'm being generous.

There was A-lot-o "F" words used in this movie and slight sexual innuendos (really one scene).

Mom wanted to protect us.

Everyone else I talked to said it was uproarious and I had to see it.

That's why "heathen" cousins with mom and dads that don't care what they watch are the best for kids like me in the situation I found myself in.

My cousins rented it and I remember starting it with my cousins, but being that they had already seen it, they were in-and-out as I sat through the entire thing, glued; frame-by-frame.

I remember smiling a lot, laughing out loud, but by the

time the film was over, I was satisfied with a very warm, happy ending for an almost begrudging relationship that the two lead characters shared throughout.

It was an underrated masterpiece that I was unaware of in my first viewing.

Damn I wish comedies could get the credit they deserve.

We open with our lead character Neal, sitting silently in a meeting, checking his watch as his superior looks over some photos for an ad campaign.

The superior shuffles through the pictures...back and forth...back and forth...back...

Neal checks his plane ticket and sees that his flight is at 6:00 and is most likely to miss it if the superior can't make a decision. Neal wants to get home for the Thanksgiving holiday.

Eventually we learn that the decision is postponed and everyone is allowed to leave.

This, of course, only upsets our lead (Neal) even more as their presence wasn't even necessary for the superior to have to come to that conclusion.

Steve Martin is the perfect Neal Page. Cynical, sarcastic, bitter, and only obsessed with his need to get home in order to keep his wife happy.

Neal has a set of obstacles (we find out later that it has only been one obstacle) set in front of him that impede him from reaching his family in time.

Enter Del Griffith (John Candy).

He is a long talking, happy-go-lucky, naïveté that has placed his luggage on the side of the street to trip up Neal from reaching his first cab. He also takes Neal's second cab while he is bickering with another would-be-cab attendant, and he ends up being his companion in coach (Neal originally had a First Class ticket, but was late and got booted) on his flight back home.

Of course the plane cannot land in Chicago...we're only 30 minutes into the movie. Due to the weather, the plane is redirected to Wichita and Neal and Del find themselves as companions on their rigorous trek back to Chicago.

Hence the title "Planes, Trains, and Automobiles" becomes extremely effective/prophetic.

Later in my life I would watch a movie that I loved called "Tommy Boy." One of my favorite comedies. "Tommy Boy's" roots are entwined in this movie. Not the overall plot and arc, but the subtle comparisons with Candy and Farley and the cynical Martin and Spade on a road trip together create a variety of contrasts and comparisons.

The first shared bed, hotel scene (and the morning after) sells this movie undoubtedly. We are first given an amazing bit of acting from Candy when he is being persecuted by Martin. His monologue retort is telling and heart-felt, swaying the audience to his side of the conundrum plot. We then get one of the most funny scenes ever put on film the next morning when the two find themselves cuddling in the queen hotel bed together.

The "between two pillows" line is the quote that is most notably remembered for this movie and rightly so. But my favorite line comes after that awkward moment.

"See that Bear's game last week?"

"Yeah, hell of a game."

John Hughes is another creator that we never give enough credit to.

He is always written off as a writer/director of the "80s teen angst melodrama," but his filmography shows so much more than that:

Director/Writer = "Sixteen Candles," "The Breakfast Club," (I know, not helping my case for someone that is more than just an 80s teen angst supporter) "Weird Science," "Ferris Bueller's Day Off," "Planes, Trains, and Automobiles," "She's Having a Baby," "Uncle Buck," and "Curly Sue." Outside of "Curly Sue," I enjoy each of these movies. His movies to me always walked on a line of absurdity, while maintaining a seriousness that justified real actions by the protagonists.

I have only mentioned the movies that he wrote/directed. He wrote original screenplays for:

ALL of the National Lampoon's Vacation movies, "Mr. Mom," "Pretty in Pink," "Some Kind of Wonderful," "The

Great Outdoors," "Career Opportunities," and "Home Alone."

It's a shame he passed at age 59. I get the feeling he had one more movie to "say something" in.

"Just like old times."-- "Yeah. You start trouble and I start bleedin'."

Before I was old enough to go hunting with my dad on open weekends, my mom and I used to stay in during the cold winters and catch a few movies together.

Shocking! I know.

We would sometimes go to the store and rent some, and sometimes we'd just sit back with a cup of coffee or hot chocolate and peruse through our inventory of copied movies.

We had a lot of movies that we would watch when we weren't sure what we were in the mood for. We'd call them "fall back" movies, now. "Jaws" was a big one and "Father Goose." There was one movie that my mom and I picked as our "no matter what" movie, however, when we kept searching and reading and suggesting and just couldn't think of any that'd hit the spot.

It was a movie that had a lot of what we liked:

- great cast
- great writing
- camaraderie
- comedy
- drama

- heroes
- damsels
- tragedy
- multiple characters doing many different things
- and redemption

It is a movie that rarely comes to mind when you mention "the greats" of all time, but if someone were to mention it as one, I wouldn't argue with them. A lot of people have never even heard about it when I mention the title, but when I tell them to go watch it, I have yet to have someone tell me they didn't enjoy it.

I might be lucky with that last bit of history, but I really feel this movie holds up over time.

"Bite the Bullet" is definitely a favorite of mine all time. Let alone a favorite western, it holds up as pure cinema to me. A lot of that probably had to do with the multiple viewings that my mom and I shared during those cold Idaho winters, but I highly recommend this film if you have never seen it.

It stars (try and catch your breath by the end of this list):

Gene Hackman, Candice Bergen, James Coburn, Ben Johnson, Jan-Michael Vincent, and Dabney Coleman makes a brief appearance.

Those are just the stars.

The people that played the supporting characters were very excellent in their roles as well including Mario Arteaga, Ian Bannen, and Walter Scott. Ian Bannen's character, Sir Harry Norfolk, has a heartbreaking scene in which I defy anyone with half-a-heart to watch without shedding a tear. The passion and pain he shared in that scene is ironed-onto my brain and won't leave, even if I want it to someday.

Mario Arteaga also comes to a very heroic, self-sacrificing end in a scene that will cause even more tears by the time you get to it.

Wow, I don't know that I'm really selling this movie...

I'll talk about the premise and you decide if it is something worth your time.

It is a western about a horse race across the desert. There are 9 people that enter the race, and we gradually learn about their character(s) in the open of the movie, prior to the race starting. We join all of them on their own separate adventures along the way. Some of their adventures intertwine and some of them don't. There are characters you love and characters you love to hate. There are even characters you love to hate that you end up loving...period; by the end. Hence the redemption that I mentioned earlier.

"Bite the Bullet," isn't just a great title or mantra for this movie. As the movie goes along, you realize how literal Richard Brooks was when he chose to run with that title.

With that last comment, you kinda *have to see it now*, right?

"Insanity doesn't run in my family, it practically gallops."

I always knew that Grant was always going to be way larger than one chapter. He is definitely on the short list of actors that deserve more than just another movie, but a list of the "bests."

So I've decided to do another "Best of," Cary Grant style.

"Topper" was the next Grant movie that I watched with my mom and sister on another weekend that my dad was gone hunting. I remember watching some scenes and having uncontrollable laughter. The premise is very creative and I don't want to give it away. Roland Young plays the title character and is the straight man through much of the film being tossed between Constance Bennett and Grant. If you like Grant and are able to find this movie, it is a must see.

"Bringing up Baby" is often times mentioned as the first or second choice of Grant fans. Rightly so. I don't know that there was a better screwball comedy duo than Cary Grant and Katharine Hepburn. Trying to explain this film would do it no justice as from start to finish, you jump from so many circumstances and so many different locations that you have to catch your breath after the first 20 minutes. Get ready to laugh, it's going to be harder to stop yourself from it.

"His Girl Friday"...Was there a better adapted screenplay in 1940? The genius move behind this movie was changing the Hildy Johnson character from a man into a woman and casting the talented Rosalind Russell. Grant and Russell are brilliant with their delivery of the dialogue here. The timing cannot be matched. Ralph Bellamy deserves a lot of credit for holding his own between these two verbal aggressors, using their phrases like sharp knives. There have been attempts to remake this movie ("Switching Channels" 1988). It was a brave effort (Christopher Reeve is the entire reason to watch this movie, taking on the role that Bellamy originally played--makes it worth a view), but the brilliance of Russel and Grant together cannot be matched. Enjoy!

"The Philadelphia Story" ...Cary Grant, Katharine Hepburn (together again), and now Jimmy Stewart...I don't know that I have to say much more. This is a movie about being honest with yourself. The honesty that rings true with Grant and Hepburn comes out in the dialogue that they share and two of the best performances of their careers is a result of that. ... Jimmy Stewart was pretty good too...

"Arsenic and Old Lace"...This is my go to Cary Grant movie. It is hands down my favorite stage play and my favorite Cary Grant movie. His slapstick, goofy facial expressions, and precise comedic dialogue timing are all on display here. He plays a man that feels he has to endure the "loonies" that *are* his family as outrageous shenanigans ensue. I dare you not to laugh.

Grant worked with some of the best directors that Hollywood has ever produced: Howard Hawks ("Bringing Up Baby" and "His Girl Friday"), George Cukor ("The

Philadelphia Story") Frank Capra ("Arsenic and Old Lace") Hitchcock ("North by Northwest," "Notorious," "To Catch a Thief") and then some....

Worth a mention: "Charade"--Great plot. The majority of the movie is Audrey Hepburn as Grant floats in and out of it. "Operation Petticoat"--Directed by Blake Edwards (one of the best comedic directors) this one kept me laughing. "The Bishop's Wife"--Plenty of Grant, not enough David Niven in my opinion, but a great heartwarming Christmas story for the holiday season.

I've given you plenty to work with...

GET TO WORK

"I don't want to hurt you! I just want to make you kosher!"

It's difficult to try and label this next movie with a genre.

If I had to, I'd definitely say it is a comedy. There are others though that would label it as a western. Like "McLintock!" I feel that it is a comedy and the American West happens to be the backdrop.

I remember this movie being one that I laughed at as a child, and that my parents laughed at as adults. That is quite a feat for a contemporary comedy (at that time) to be able to throw enough adult humor in, and not cross the line so that your children can enjoy it with you.

That is what I remember doing. Watching "The Frisco Kid" with my parents, multiple times.

The gist:

A Polish rabbi, Avram ([Gene Wilder](#)) has been chosen to run a synagogue in San Francisco, CA. He takes a boat from Poland to Philadelphia, PA where he runs into a small group of bandits that rob him and throw him alongside the road. Beaten down, he is however determined to get to San Francisco.

Along the way he runs into the Amish who aid him, works along the railroad line for enough money to buy a horse and supplies, and eventually he runs in with his guardian "angel," Tommy (a very young and wily [Harrison Ford](#)).

* * *

To divulge on the history and character of Tommy would spoil you of some effective storytelling. Let's agree that he is a man that knows who he is.

The majority of the humor comes from Gene Wilder's Avram.

His thick accent is quite humorous, and his uncanny world view on doing the right thing without judging others is a characteristic to envy in such a goofy protagonist. There is also some major culture clash along the way that sets up some funny situations when Tommy's style and Avram's beliefs don't see eye-to-eye.

The trek across the old American West is quite a major one, and Michael Elias and Frank Shaw did a great job of showing the common difficulties of that journey in their screenplay.

It is nice to watch a very young Ford fresh off his fame from Star Wars interact in a comedy with the brilliant timing of Gene Wilder. I feel that Ford learned a lot on this picture and shows his comedy skills (even in moments of his dramas) after this movie debuted in 1979.

For me I will always remember this as a movie we watched as a family when we wanted a laugh. There are a lot of them, and watching Wilder carry a picture was a joy. It's a shame he's not seen much anymore. Great talent.

"I'm a kid that's my job."

We watched this next one as a family. Everyone except my sister. She was a very busy high school student, had a lot of after school activities, and then came home and studied (she graduated in the top 10 in her class-- nerd alert!)

This was one of those movies that I wish she could've been there with us to see for the first time. Her perspective would've gone a long way.

I always like to call it the forgotten John Hughes gem.

This was another of our "fall back" movies. My dad and I probably watched this movie together over 10 times. He was always game for it.

I don't think anyone would meet a bigger John Candy fan than my father, and "Uncle Buck" was probably his favorite "Candy Movie."

The gist: There is a family "health emergency" and the parents of the family have to go and attend to it (mom's grandfather is very sick and has almost died)...However, they know that it could be a very extended period of time that they will need to be gone and the kids cannot miss that amount of school. They try EVERYONE and the only option--dad's deadbeat-jobless-never-invited-to-Thanksgiving-dinner-brother, "Buck" Russell.

It's unfortunate that there was only one movie. The character Candy was able to make out of "Buck" always seemed to be larger than just one movie. I thought it would've been awesome to see Buck come back to save the day when the youngest daughter got into high school too. There would've been a different dynamic, given that he had a good relationship with her as an adolescent, but at the end of the day, she still would've been a teenager....

I digress.

Long story short, Buck is great with the young children, he clashes major with the teenage daughter:

Buck: "When I was his age, I was a guy zooming girls like you. Pretty face, good chip on your shoulder."

The funniest scenes in the movie come from Buck tormenting the teenager's (Tia's) boyfriend, "Bug."

To spoil you of seeing how Buck torments Bug for the first time would be foul play on my part. Trust me, there are laugh-out-loud moments, that have a level of discomfort to go along with them.

I remember talking with my dad on our third or fourth viewing about whether or not he would do those things.

Dad: "For my niece? You bet I would."

Me: "Niece? What about Beth?"

(Beth is my sister)

Dad: "I don't need to worry about your sister, she'd be

meaner to those boys than me or Buck ever could be."

That statement is no bullshit. My dad prepared my sister very well. One of the most independent people I know. Again, I would've loved to ask her about her impressions of the Tia character from a teenage girl's point-of-view. It would've been very interesting. Tia isn't a bad person, she was just an angry teenager. Who hasn't been one at some point?

The great thing about the conflict in the movie between Buck and Tia, is that I can see both sides to the argument. Buck has been tasked with keeping his niece safe and does it in the only way he knows how; understanding the male teenager mind. Tia uses what Buck has become as an adult against him. Buck's not the most eligible bachelor, being that he is closer to 50 than 40 and unemployed with no prospects. Not the best example to be giving out strict orders to a rebellious teen.

We have another brilliant screenplay by the amazing John Hughes, and an actor that was born for this role. Candy is very underrated as an actor in general. Most people right him off as a large clown. Movies like this and "[Planes, Trains, and Automobiles](#)" prove otherwise.

The greatness with a lot of the dialogue is how Buck engages with the young children too. He is gentle, but he treats and communicates with them like they are his equal. He doesn't try to talk down to them or make them feel that they do not have a voice too. He is a good listener and acknowledges the things they have to contribute.

* * *

I have an "Uncle Buck" in my family too (in moments, I feel I have more than one). I like to believe that everyone does. For those of you that don't, I feel a little sorry for you. "Uncle Bucks" make family gatherings very interesting....

....and authentic...

"Hey, man, are you all right?" -- "Yeah, I'll die soon, then it'll all be over..."

My father passed away in August of 2013. There have been a few of these posts that have been difficult for me. "The Cowboys" and "Field of Dreams" come to mind.

This one will be another challenge.

Every time I think of this next movie, I think of my dad. We were only able to watch it together one time, unfortunately. I think that the reason being was that it was hard for him to watch it with other people.

He was a man that had a hard time letting go of his past self. I might be reading into this (I'm sure I'm going to hear it from my sister if she happens upon this), but it is how I feel.

Make no mistake, even though we only saw it one time together, my father L-O-V-E-D this movie.

My mom and my uncles used to tell me stories about my dad's 67 cherry red GTO that he used to "rod" and race when he was in high school. It had a 400 in it and he had a pair of brass knuckles for the handle of the manual gear shift.

I was told he loved it.

My father was a man of few words and if someone else

was willing to talk about it while he was in the room, he'd let them. I used to look over at him when other people were telling *his* stories. He always had a mischievous grin under his big beard as he listened sitting in his chair with his arms crossed.

He used to talk about what a mistake it was to ever let that GTO go.

"Man, I could kick myself," he'd say.

As it pertains to "American Graffiti" I always felt that my dad was reliving his own life when that VHS was spooling through the machine that projected those images of the cars driving around that town in that movie.

It wasn't just the racing that brought him back (there's really only one quick scene). It was the culture that was relived in that movie. I can't think of a movie off hand that knew it's own tone better than this one, and it never surrenders that message throughout.

The dialogue alone gave my dad flashbacks:

"Oh, rats."

"Don't you think the Beach Boys are boss?"

"Hey, man, who cut the cheese?"

"...it only took me one night to realize if brains were dynamite you couldn't blow your nose."

* * *

People don't talk like that any more. The "assumed innocence" that oozed from the 1960s bled out all over the screen after George Lucas created "American Graffiti."

For my father, this was as nostalgic for him as "Ferris Bueller's Day Off," "War Games," "Back to the Future," etc. were for me.

I think that as much as he enjoyed it, he wanted to watch it alone where he could reminisce in his own mind.

I remember randomly taking some looks back at my father as he would watch on and he had some tears in his eyes, in moments through the film that seemed out of place. I think that the movie just moved him very closely and "took him back"...and he knew he really couldn't "go back."

Later I remembered asking my dad why he got rid of his red GTO.

"Well son, I wanted to get married and have a family. That wasn't a family car and as much as I miss it, I'd never keep that damn thing if it meant I couldn't have you guys."

As I sit writing this and choking back some tears, I remember thinking how corny that sounded to me when I was in junior high. All it does is make me want to cry now. Looking back, it was a rare moment where my father was trying to have an honest conversation with me about how he felt. Now that I have a son of my own,

I understand it.

At the end of the day, "American Graffiti" is a great movie that I will watch hopefully many more times before I pass.

I love the atmosphere, the dialogue, and the "young" actors (Ron Howard, Richard Dreyfuss, Cindy Williams, Charles Martin Smith, and Harrison Ford) that had the energy and zeal that this 1960s portrayal needed.
Trying to explain scenes and plot points in this movie would not only do it injustice, it would confuse the hell out of everyone.

I remember when my parents first rented it. I asked them what it was about and they couldn't really explain it. They just kept saying, "It's about the 60s," and "You'll just have to watch it."

We did watch it...

...and they were right.

"Are you one of them?" -- "One of What?"

I was 11 and I was a good listener.

My mom used to talk about movies with my "adopted aunt" Jo Lynn and I'd drop some eaves (thank you Samwise for one of my favorite phrases).

I should mention, my family was a huge Kevin Costner fan...

Okay...my mom was a huge Kevin Costner fan so *my* family was a huge Kevin Costner fan, right?

So there was a period of time where all we rented was another Costner movie after another Kevin Costner movie...not complaining. This was when they were good.

Yes. There was a period of time when that happened. It's called the late 80s circa early 90s...then he made "Robin Hood: Prince of Thieves" (as if we didn't know that green hooded asshole was the "prince of thieves")

Colons don't belong in movie titles. They belong in three places:

1. Before a list (See the irony here?)
2. Between the hour and the minutes, and
3. Between our cecum and our rectum (toilet joke, you're welcome!)

...

* * *

Where the hell am I?

Oh, yeah...so I overheard my mom talking to my aunt about this movie and she went on and on and on about how, "wonderful" it was and, "what a great story," and how it "forced her to pay attention," and that she was glad that she did pay attention.

I was intrigued.

So I asked my mom later about it.

"What was that movie you were talking about?"

Mom: "Huh?"

"With Jo Lynn. You said it was a great movie."

Looked at me like she might need me to get tested for a mental illness.

I sighed and rolled my eyes. I didn't want to say it but, "It had Kevin Costner in it."

Mom: "OH! It's called No Way Out...you can't watch it."

Typical.

I expected this reaction (I was used to it) so I had to keep it cool and work on her.

This was the first movie that mom REALLY caved on. By the end of that day with my nagging, she made it happen and we watched it that weekend. I secretly think she really wanted to watch it again with me and get my opinion. If you think about it, she got to watch a great movie again, and she got see my reaction to a very intelligent twister of a movie. Sometimes watching a movie with your kids for the first time and hoping that they'll share in your joy and reaction is better than your first viewing.

I think that happened with mom on this one.

I sincerely remember having my first "WHAAAAAAAAAT" moment by the end of that tense movie.

I learned about "plot." How important it really is and how interesting "plot" can be.

I think I watched it three times that year.

I also learned a little more about the female anatomy (thank you younger Sean Young)...the first time I watched it with mom those scenes were fastforwarded. In a weird way the fastforwarding made the sex scenes more awkward to watch with your mother if you can imagine that. It makes it look way more painful than anything and sometimes you cut off the beginning of a crucial scene and you had to rewind and then you were in the middle of the sex scene again and you had to fastforward and mom got stressed out and pushed the buttons harder than she needed to....

It amused me.

* * *

"No Way Out" is another one of those movies that I don't want to mention regarding the story because that would be taking away a very good moment for you if you have never heard of it or seen it.

Go watch it. It'll deliver.

Oh, except the very cheesy 80s electric piano score...try and block that out.

Other than that distraction, #Great movie!

"Women and children can afford to be careless, but not men."

I have a confession.

I love this next movie. From time to time in my life I have told people that it is my favorite movie.

...and...

I have avoided writing about it.

I mean, how do you write about your favorite movie? It has to be perfect, right? You have to know everything about it--inside and out--and you have to have seen it at least 10 times. I feel that I have accomplished that, but I found myself having a difficult time putting into words all of the reasons that I love it...and there are many. I thought I'd do what I always do.

Talk about my family.

So there are two phases with this movie. There is the first time that I've heard about it and the first time that I watched it.

I'll start with the first time that I heard about it.

I had a friend named Rob that used to play "jam ball" with me when we were in junior high. For those of you that don't know what "jam ball" is, it's when a bunch of short people that will never be able to "jam" a basketball on a 10' hoop decide to go to an elementary school play ground and "jam" on an 8' hoop.

If you haven't tried it, don't judge. It's fun to feel like a real basketball player sometimes.

Any way, on a Friday, we ended up going to my house and Rob was going to stay overnight. When we walked to my house mom had rented a movie and she was so excited to sit and watch it. I could tell by the way she said the title. It was like it changed the atmosphere of the room when she spoke it, and everyone knew what she was talking about when she said it...everyone...except me.

"What's 'The Godfather,'" I asked with a raised eyebrow.

Without hesitation Rob said, "It's about the mafia."

I looked at him like he was speaking Aramaic.

"What's the mafia?"

"Organized crime," my mom said.

It was a brief conversation that I ignored at the time as Rob and I ended up playing out in the yard for most of the evening after dinner.

I do remember pausing with Rob at the tv as we watched the movie briefly on our walk to my bedroom for bed.

There was a car that exploded...

* * *

Awesome. (I found out later that it wasn't so awesome...)

My curiosity was peaked and a week later I was asking my mom if she would let me rent that again. I wanted to know what everyone else knew....

...and the car bomb was pretty cool.

Mom agreed as long as she could watch it with me again. I didn't care, I was glad to.

I learned a lot of things about the movie watching it with my mom for the first time. Number one, it was a book. A book that my mom owned, read a couple of times, and loved. I also learned a lot of "inside book reader" information that my mom had and shared with me throughout the movie, in particular, there is a scene where Michael takes out a handkerchief and wipes his nose when he is in Sicily talking with his bodyguards and sees his future first wife Apollonia for the first time. Mom would pause the movie and explain to me that Michael had chronic nose bleeds ever since Captain McCluskey punched him in the face breaking his eye socket bone, outside of the hospital the night he saved the Don's life. These are the kind of details that you get in the book and the movie made subtle decisions to keep those details in it without using dialogue to explain everything.

That's just one example. Mom had many throughout.

I remember the tension the movie had starting with the first monologue. It took a little break to get through the wedding, then each scene after the next felt like it was slowly clenching a fist and after the first jab when Luca Brasi gets viciously murdered, the movie is a series of plots, political discussions and brutal murders during wartime in an organized crime underground that seeps out into the front page of the newspapers.

...and that's just the tone of the movie.

The cast became legends after this movie. Brando first, then Caan, Pacino, Duvall, and Keaton.

The story has many different levels to it. Really it is about one generation keeping what they have and making sure that the future of the next generation is secure. Along the way there are choices made by many characters that have extreme consequences in their world. It is a world full of danger, confidence, bravado, tragedy, horror, and triumph.

I really feel that I would've loved this movie regardless, but there was something about watching it with my mother and her commentary that made it mean more. Her love for the story and the characters made it a deeper viewing experience for me. This added to the enjoyment of a great story and had an influence on how I viewed stories thereafter.

My dad liked the car bombs.

"Someone is staring at you in 'personal growth'."

This next one is similar to "Roxanne" and "Splash."

No, Daryl Hannah isn't in it, but it is considered a comedy romance.

A pretty good comedy romance. Some people'd say *great* and I wouldn't disagree with them.

Personally, it's not a "go to" genre for me. Most guys that I know don't have that as their favorite genre either, but I do like a well written, witty, comedy romance, and this one delivers.

At that stage in my life, a lot of the comedy romance movies that I'd seen and enjoyed had one of two things-- slapstick/screwball ("Roxanne," "Bringing up Baby") or goofy fantasy ("Splash").

This one was different. It was mostly dialogue between two people at a time (sometimes 3 or 4 people at most). I found that I really had to pay attention to what people were saying to each other in order to gain an interest and an understanding of the story that the writers were trying to tell. There was little movement or action unless people were walking and talking.

It was unlike any type of movie that I was used to or had viewed, yet I found myself surprisingly captivated.

I remember watching it with my mom and sister for the

first time and I began understanding what "adult" humor was: wit, sarcasm, timing, and circumstance. It was the first time I started laughing at the same time they laughed instead of just laughing because they laughed, like I had learned to do when I was seven or eight. I actually understood the jokes and found it funny like they did.

In those other comedies I was learning *when* to laugh. By the time I had seen this one, I was *ready* to laugh.

And laugh I did when I watched "When Harry Met Sally" for the first time.

I found that as I watched it, my mom and sister enjoyed Sally's point of view and I was of course fond of Harry's cynicism (take in mind I didn't know what *cynicism* was at that time but I was learning quickly that I enjoyed his "mood.")

Sally was cute and annoying (it takes her 5 minutes to order lunch and she is an unapologetic optimist). Harry was short, goofy looking, and didn't like anyone or anything. Perfect matches right?

Looking back, I should've known better (SPOILER-of course they will end up together-IT'S A COMEDY ROMANCE!!!). Again, this was one of the first CRs that I'd actually sat through and I wasn't jaded at this point with *all* of the formulaic CRs to follow. I think that is why I enjoyed it so much. I view it as my first true Rom-Com and I was young enough for it to be a surprise for me as the story and conflict developed.

* * *

I'm stretching a grin across my face as I write this, remembering how naive I was when Harry trudges over to Sally on New Year's Eve and berates her at the party like he wants to start another war and then it turns into one of the greatest "I love you speeches" ever written. I seriously remember thinking, "Oh yeah, so they are going to get together. Huh...look at that."

This might be the Comedy Romance that ruined the genre for me, actually, because it is the one that I compare the rest to and you can never have a surprise after you have seen your first formula Rom-Com.

Apologies to anyone that has read this before seeing it. I know that I haven't been my usual cryptic self while writing about a movie I enjoyed, but it was exciting for me to finally give something away.

Almost as exciting as watching a well written Comedy Romance for the first--as a naive youth--time.

"Where about you from?"

There are movies that make you say, "Who's that?"

You look them up on the back of a movie case in a rental store and attempt to find every movie that they have made prior and all of those movies that will follow.

That movie for me was "Glory."

That person was Denzel.

I was unprepared for the pure power and emotion of the performance he put forth. He came from out of nowhere for me and he seemed like a seasoned movie star that stole every scene he was in, leaving all of us to wish that he was in every frame.

It was the first movie I'd seen him in and I later rented "[The Mighty Quinn](#)." He was in every frame of that great thriller and the film love affair began.

Thank God for "Glory."

Not only was it my intro to Denzel, it had [Ferris Bueller](#) and [Westley](#) in it too. It was unlike any other movie I'd seen about war. The first battle doesn't even take place until well over an hour into the movie. It had a very "All Quiet on the Western Front" feel to it. It was about the soldiers "boots" on the ground versus the two sided perspectives you'd see in a war. The confederate soldiers were ominous, almost ghost-like when they appear out of the smoke and fog during the first battle.

It is one of the most eerie scenes depicted in a war movie that I've had the pleasure of experiencing. The confederates don't really have faces or perspectives for us to draw from. Their purpose is opposition and nothing more.

Labeling "Glory" as a Civil War drama is misguided. It is that, but it is also a story about brotherhood on a very interesting and dysfunctional level. Part of the journey we take with this story is watching the growth of a unit of men by the films end.

When I think of the movie--outside of it being my thankful introduction to Denzel--I remember the unexpected, deep true power I felt of those last few frames of the soldiers being bundled together in the ground.

Much like there are moments of struggle and choices that we learn from in life, in the end we have the people that stick through it with us in the toughest of times.

Yes, friends fight; and if they can see it through, they become best friends or the brothers that we get to choose. We all have mentors that teach us. Some of them become the fathers that we have always wanted to respect and love.

"It's not exactly a normal world, is it?"

In the 80s, my exposure to Batman looked something like this:

(Imagine a picture of the animated "Super Friends" version of Batman and Robin here. *See author's note)

In 1988, they started rerunning "Batman" in syndication on our local CBS affiliate. Adam West and Burt Ward were the leads as the "Dynamic Duo," and I didn't tell any of my friends that I made sure I watched EVERY episode.

I remember every villain was given two episodes each. The first always left our heroes in peril. As you can imagine, Friday on the first run was the worst, I had to wait until Monday to find out how they were going to escape.

The point?

Batman stories on film and television were effing campy. That all changed in 1989.
Tim Burton was fresh off his early success with "Beetlejuice" and was building momentum with his adaptation of the Caped Crusader.

Michael Keaton brought us a very different Bruce Wayne/Batman. Batman used to race to the scene, jump in the middle, and thump the villain with his fists. He'd also announce every "bat-weapon" before he used it. Keaton's portrayal was elusive and in the shadows. Burton and Keaton knew that less would be more when he wore the Bat-suit and it worked.

I enjoyed how intimidating the look of Batman was. There had to be a realistic discussion about how a man *could* be the Batman and the creators of this version had to agree that the psychological power of the legend of Batman was how a man *could* be Batman. The look had to be scary opposed to the "friendly neighborhood bat" that we were all used to, since he was going to be someone that had to scare, frightening street thugs and villains.

Speaking of...Jack is still my favorite Joker. I have nothing against Heath Ledger, Cesar Romero, and I am excited to see what Jared Leto is going to bring, but Jack made me laugh out loud when he was doing terrible things. That might speak to my personal "issues," however, I find that thrilling.

Jack's Joker for me is up there with Jerry Dandridge and Darth Vader...villains that you root for a little bit. Villains, that when they die at the end of a movie, you realize that the amusement ride has just ended and now you have to unbuckle and stumble out of the cart.

The soundtrack also features music from the one and only Prince (RIP). His track "Trust" that plays when the Joker comes out on his float throwing out trash bags of money to the masses is perfect and still one of my favorite "movie-moment" songs.

I was dropped off at the theater with my cousin to see

this movie. We went on the second weekend and arrived 15 minutes early. After we got our tickets and entered the theater, we had to sit 4th row back from the screen. On its second run, theaters were still packed. Like it or not, this new version of Batman was a hit and audiences loved Burton's vision of what Gotham's lonely hero could become.

"Batman" would be the last movie I would see in theaters from the 1980s. I couldn't be sure what to expect from the 90s in film, but"Batman" has become my bridge between those decades. You'd think I'm a 1980s homer when it comes to movie viewing, but just wait. I'm going to love sharing some of the movies that inspired me through the 1990s, which turned out to be my favorite decade.

Worthy Unmentionables

When it comes to film, I do love the 80s...I could probably just write about the 80s for the rest of my life. There are *that* many good movies. We all move on though, sometimes out of necessity and I have to give the 90s a shot too (I'm actually excited to do that since that's my favorite decade--more on that later).

I thought it only fair to give some of the movies that I love that I didn't have time for to get a little #ShoutOut.

"Harry and the Hendersons" is a very underrated and often forgotten 1980s family movie. It has one of my top 10 favorite actors of all time the #Great John Lithgow, and the puppet effects that were used to create a warm hearted "Bigfoot Monster" were well ahead of their time. Lithgow is a great actor because he is comfortable in high drama, horror, farce, and family comedy. His performance is what makes this film so believable about a dad who wants to keep his family safe, but he wants to teach them about protecting your friends as well. It's streaming on Netflix now and I just watched it with my son. He couldn't stop laughing.

How cool would it be if our *Legend of Zelda* scores allowed us to go back in time to another dimension, become Link, and save the princess from the evil Gannon? "The Last Strarfighter" has a similar premise. Alex is a bored teenager with big dreams who happens to be the highest score on the local *Starfighter* arcade game. Little does he know that game is a test and he has to save the Universe from a galactic empire. I found it intriguing, entertaining, and yet another example of an

80s movie building up their children to save the world.

What if we could learn how to do anything? ...Okay, we kinda can. What if we could learn how to do anything...in 30 seconds. "D. A. R. Y. L." is about an android that gets adopted into a family and has to learn who he was, where he is from, and what he needs to become. There's really not a whole lot to the story other than a few cool set pieces. What's great about it is how it makes the impossible seem possible for the children yet again in this strange world we all live in. He might save the day...not giving it away.

It's been well documented that I love John Hughes. Here's another Hughes film that seems a little sexist...and then we meet Lisa and it's all good...okay, it's still a bit sexist, but I do find this movie entertaining. Basically, two geeky high school kids that only have each other set out to create the "perfect woman." SEXIST--they end up creating Lisa played by Kelly Lebrock and what you might think happens next, does not. I find it hilarious, silly, and in the end, warm and entertaining like all Hughes films. Check it out.

"Real Genius" is the movie that introduced us to Val Kilmer. Don't get me wrong, "Top Secret" was great, but Kilmer's true acting genius (See what I did there?) was on full display in this film. How do you play the smartest person in the world? Are they quirky? What genius isn't? We've all seen interviews with Steve Jobs and heard the stories about Thomas Edison only needing 2 hours of sleep at night. Quirks galore come out in this movie and everyone should experience it without knowing much about it their first time. Go see it. It will deliver.

The atmosphere that was created in "To Live and Die in L. A." is what makes it brilliant, but what also might have made it less desirable at the box office. This is not your average cop thriller by any means. I have seen nothing like it and I don't want to. It is a thrilling masterpiece; original and couldn't pump the breaks if it wanted to. The different themes that the creators explore about obsession, art, greed, and revenge are enthralling and tragic. It's a tough one to find, but well worth the effort. Friedkin is a true auteur that is comfortable in this genre (The French Connection) and has upped the ante with thrilling "chases" in this picture. Find it. Watch it. Watch it again.

In the 80s, if I watched a trailer that had a hero with a sword in it, I didn't care if it was good, I had to see it. Such was the case with "The Black Cauldron." I remember seeing the commercial, telling my mom, and seeing it opening weekend with my mom, my little brother, my best friend, and her mom. We were not ready for how dark and scary this Disney animated feature was going to be. It is engaging, well crafted, thrilling, and not given the respect it deserves amongst the best Disney Films over the decades. I try and watch it once a year...for nostalgia and because the villains in it have depth for a Disney picture creating a very intriguing atmosphere.

I know I've probably left some out. I know that I will get a lot of shit for not writing about "Fletch." You need to understand, I didn't see "Fletch" for the first time until last year. Sorry. Others that I liked: "The

Untouchables," "Dead Poets Society," "Escape from New York," and "Better Off Dead."

Believe it or not, there are still some very cult classic 1980s movies that are still on my list to see: "Something Wild," "Local Hero," "Angel Heart," and "The Brave Little Toaster." I will see all of these before I die...I've said that to myself a lot and haven't got around to it. If I hit 50 and am still saying this, I'm going to start to worry.

So, goodbye 80s. I loved you, but the 90s is going to get their fair share too. We'll also start to see some classic movies (30s, 40s, 50s, 60s, 70s) hit the upcoming blog posts as I started going to college in the mid 90s and my taste in film changed and became more educated. We are saying goodbye, but you will always be there. Without you 80s, I wouldn't have a film foundation to draw from as I watched older films. That equals a very special place in my heart. Thank you.

Thank you...

....for using your precious time to read my silly stories about me and my quirky family. My hope is that you enjoyed my film viewing history. There are plenty more to come and your support will help them come even faster. If you have a few moments more, please add a quick, honest review on Amazon or any other format that you are more comfortable with.

#Clintington's debut fiction project, Get Back is available on Amazon; November 2016.

So, here is a sneak peek of the first chapter of my first novel, Get Back. I hope you enjoy it:

(1)
Matthew Bryerson

December, 1996

That scrawny looking guy that looks out of place amongst all of these people having a good time. That's me. Not the one that lost his map to math lab and took a wrong turn, *he is wearing a sweet orange vest though over that nice collared long-sleeve black shirt. Go B's!* The other guy standing next to him with the beer in his hand; the guy with the glasses and the short ratty hair, that's me. I'm the host of this god awful festival if you can believe that. Look at all of those debauched little fools dancing around like its Mardi Gras. Well, at least I get to make sure the music is good at my own party. Once "Free Bird" hits the ears I know that it is time to jet. You won't hear that shit kick'n' piss tonight. Look at all those assholes and elbows banging together to some alternative tune that half of these people don't understand the words to or recognize. They have no concept of who the artist is, the name of the song, or why the poet wrote it. All they know is that it has a good beat to slam into each other with in unison so that no one falls over and gets trampled. I enjoy this kind of music for different reasons. Right now I just want to listen to the words and try to understand why this song is speaking to me in this moment. I don't know why he titled it after an anti-manic drug. Maybe it was because that is how he felt after taking it. Maybe that is how he thought he might feel if he took it, who knows? "*...happy...lonely...day...daze....*" Every time I hear it, I try to see myself doing and being those things that he describes. I never can relate it to mood altering medications, though since I've never taken them. Besides, I think an upper would be more appropriate. I might act like these guys and enjoy myself.

I used to have fun at these things, but lately I don't have that much to cheer about. Now, before I continue, I'm writing this so you get a perspective of what it's like to be an average guy digging through a trough. I've hit some peaks, but as I write this, I tend to be in what I am hoping is a small gutter with low flow.

That girl's alone. I should go talk to her. I hate this part. This is the shit that I have never been good at. She's alone and waiting and I'm bumbling around with my hand in my pocket trying to think of something clever to say.
Oh, man. Asshole spilt beer all over me!

I didn't need that. It's one thing to be witless and dry, the wetness adds an anxious bonus. Now, before I take this plunge, I should probably give you a little back-story so that you get to know me before I make a total and complete jackass of myself while trying to woo this innocent girl with my evil man powers.

Four months ago my life changed...

September, 1996

I woke up to an empty bed and my unhappy girlfr—ex-girlfriend—was packing the remaining portion of her stuff. What the hell, right? Well, I kind of saw it coming, but no one—I'm talking no one—wants to go through what those days offer. So I got up and watched her finish packing. Yes, it was stressful and I did take my glasses off and rub my temples. You'll find that I do that a lot when I am trying to think of something clever to say.

She just kept packing that damn box and didn't act like I was even there. The packing kept getting louder and louder with each object that hit the bottom of that box.

Thump! Thump! THUMP! THUMP!

"Don't go. Please, I know how hard it is to live with me."

That's about as clever as it gets when I am stalling—pathetic, but honest.

She just kept packing that goddamn box as if I had not said anything at all.

THUMP! THUMP!

"Just...Can we talk some more?"

THUMP! THUMP!

"I know we hashed the hell out of this but...."

THUMP! THUMP!

"COULD YOU STOP PACKING FOR A SECOND AND LISTEN TO ME?!"

THUMP, went one more item as she crossed her arms and glared at me. I may have come on a little strong with that last request, but I got the result. It was probably the first time I had her full attention in the last six months.

"Thank you."

I had to stop and think for a second before I lit the fuse.

"Now I refuse to believe that this entire time that we've been together you weren't happy. How can you be with someone seven years and not tell them that you're unhappy?"

Question of fucking Questions if you ask me.

"We had fun." *PRESENT TENSE, PRESENT TENSE!* "We *have* fun." I stumbled over that one.

"I love Thursday mornings."

On Thursdays, we alternated making breakfast in bed for each other. We hadn't missed a Thursday in the seven years we lived together.

"You're a great cook."

Lie.

"That's our catch up day. I love breakfast. I . . . I love you."

Stalling again.

"Don't you see that? Now, I know that I am miserable, but I have always loved you. You're the only one I've been with since high school. If that ain't love, I don't know what is."

You can't see her face right now, but she is mentally slitting my throat; bad time for a joke.

"Seven years. Do you really believe we've been wasting our time? We can work it out."

When she stood up and picked up that box, my heart

crushed my balls.

"You seem content. But, if you ever had a feeling at all that we weren't doomed from the beginning, you'll empty that box and talk to me. But if you leave, that means you never *really* loved me. It was just words every time you said it." *Heartless manipulation, I know, but she was leaving with the last box.*

There was a blissful moment there when I looked up into her eyes and I thought for a split second that I had her, but her mind was made up. When she slammed the door behind her, it was a slap to the face. I got up and had to say something. "Seven fucking years!" I shouted at her. "What a cliché!"

It's unfortunate that I *am* one of those "has-to-have-the-last-word" kind of guys. Even though she didn't say anything the whole time, that door slam was louder than any of those expletives I yelled at her. So I tried to slam the door louder than her a couple of times, but it just never seemed to get as loud as hers no matter how much force I put into it.

I don't remember a lot of the details that day, except when I broke the news to my "friend(s)". You have to tell someone. They'll find out eventually and it's just better to get it off your chest. It was after practice, and I had a *shitty* practice. Everyone noticed. My best friend Billy sat down next to me after practice when we were taking our cleats and shin-guards off. I only had what happened with Randy on my mind, as you can imagine.

"Whew, I am one sweaty bastard," he said. "I think that was all right for me any way. You okay?"

No, my girlfriend left me. How are you?

I really said, "Randy left me."

I thought that he was going to throw up. I guess that's how best friends react.

"Fuck you, serious?" he asked.

I just gave him a look and he understood *how* serious I was.

"Fuck, sorry man. What happened?"

I was surprised by all the expletives. He doesn't curse a lot—especially with the "for unlawful carnal knowledge" word. I didn't know that I had it in me to make him swear so much.

I couldn't answer his question. I needed more time to think about it, but I didn't particularly want to be alone, either.

"Let's go to Emery's and we'll talk about it. I don't want to do it here."

Just a side note, Emery's is my favorite sports bar. Wonderful food, any beer you want, and—it's locally owned so there are no corporate douche bags worried about sales and expanding. *Fucking Cheers man.*

Anyways, as I invited Billy to the bar, I didn't notice the tall drinks of water standing behind me; Davy and Brock. I would call them friends, but with friends like these—well, I guess all best friends give each other shit, that's why they're your *best* friends. Musketeer wise, Davy is to Aramis as Brock is to Porthos as Billy is to Athos. Yeah, I'm fucking d'Artagnan. I'm telling the story, I'm d'Artagnan.

So, not noticing them, they heard "Emery's" and their ears perked up.

"Emery's? I'm down," said Brock.

Before I could say anything, Billy blabbed, "Randy left him."

"Fuck off man. Serious?" asked Davy.

I couldn't describe the look I threw Billy. I don't think he felt comfortable with his back facing me the rest of that evening.

"Well, let's go get some pizza bombs," suggested Brock.

"And beer," Davy added as he looked at me and shook his head. "Shit man."

We made it across the street and started talking after we sat and ordered our food. I was definitely ready for sympathy night, but Brock and Davy weren't selling.

"She basically told me she never *really* loved me," I continued. "I know I'm a fucking asshole, but come on, I made some sacrifices for her."

That was the point at which I hoped the conversation would lead to my "friends" reminding me of *all* the sacrifices I did indeed actually make, but they weren't going to tug on that line.

"Like what," asked Brock.

I wanted to knock the smug bastard off the back of his bar stool.

"Like staying here instead of trying out," I quickly reminded him. "I went to school because she wanted me to. I wanted to go try out for the *Foxes*...didn't happen...I stayed here for her."

"You were *really* going to try out?" asked Davy, raised eyebrow in tow.

What the fuck?

"YES...as sure as you're sitting there."

I couldn't let him think that I wouldn't.

"So go try out now man, you're free," said a positive (and appreciated) Billy.

"Next year man. I missed this year. Next year."

Brock shook his head wearing a pompous smile, "I think that's your problem right there."

"What?" I asked.

"You're always putting shit off. There's no decision making, just excuses."

"Nice Brock," said Billy.

At the same time I said, "What the fuck man?"

All Brock could muster at that point was, "Hey, I'm just saying."

My steam whistle was getting ready to go off.

"Do you have to say it now? Dickhead! My girlfriend just left me after seven fucking years. The only woman I've ever been with."

All three of them sipped their beer and ate their pizza. I lost my appetite. It was very uncomfortable. Davy broke the silence.

"Brock makes a good point though."

"Don't encourage him," said Billy.

Davy replied, "No, hear me out."

He looked at me and smiled, I didn't want to hear what he had to say, but I knew I was going to.

Davy continued, "When *did* you finally declare a major?"

Low blow.

Everyone knew I didn't want to be in school, so how the hell was I supposed to pick a major. I replied honestly.

"When I had to."

I wanted to call *him* a dickhead, but I don't think he would have heard me.

"How many times did you switch majors?"

The fucking questions! I just wanted them to eat and leave.

"Five times."

I couldn't look at them. I just looked up at one of the televisions and drank my beer. I didn't care what was on; it could've been "Beverly Hills 90210" for all I cared. I wasn't going to look at those assholes.

I could feel their eyes on me for a split second. I know those two bastards shared a smug glance with each other.

Discomfort.

Damn silence.

"What kind of friends would we be if we didn't point out the obvious," asked Davy.

At least the douche bag broke the awful silence.

"The kind that do it later," said Billy.

I could have kissed him. He took the words right out of my mouth.

He continued, "Like not the day that someone's been fucked over. I know he's an asshole—hell he does."

"I do," I said.

Please continue sir.

"It doesn't mean he needs to hear this shit right now from you assholes."

They ARE assholes! I don't know why I hang out with those two.

"Well he needs to hear this," Brock spouted off.

"I'm sitting right here," I wanted to hit him. No one likes it when they're being talked about like they're not there.

"You need to hear this," agreed Davy.

Motherfucker! I want to kick his ass too.

"You guys are out of line," said Billy.

Speechless for too long, I got sick of the silence. I did what every guy I know does when he is having a conversation that is going nowhere and he no longer wants to have it.

"I gotta take a piss."

And I did.

I didn't see it, but I imagine Billy shook his head like he always does when he's disgusted beyond words.

I don't think I'd do that to them if they were in this circumstance. I don't think they know better....but sometimes, friends feel that being self-righteous is the only way to be a *true* friend. That's Brock and Davy.

So the day after my friends reminded me of what an asshole *I* was, we had a game. The game was not one to be remembered, but what I do recall was very interesting—I "shared a moment" with someone at that game.

Okay, that sounds weird, I know, but I'm banking on it's not what you think. I'm not the kind of guy to get sappy and write about what a wonderful, kooky experience I had and how it changed my life for the better. As much as it changed me, I don't have a gift of visions where I go from town-to-town helping people change their futures. *Like Kane from "Kung fu"...that would be badass*—but...no, not that kind of "moment." I don't write those stories. I write what I know and I know that it was a perception, but it was a little more selfish than the average, uh, "gift." That's probably why I don't write those kinds of stories. Yet again, we are aware that I'm an asshole; well established.

I remember the whistle clear as day as the ref called a foul on Billy for tackling from behind. The next thing I know me, Davy, Billy and Brock are setting up the "wall". Davy was on my left facing the ball. Billy was on my right facing the ball. Brock was next to Davy with his back to the ball as he looked to our keeper for directions.

I always get jazzed up when I'm standing in the wall. It is one of the few experiences in life that can be generally physically painful, but emotionally rewarding at the same time. It was different that day, my mind wasn't in the game. I remember looking into the stands for any sign of Randy.

I also felt that was a *great* moment to share my pain and frustration aside to Billy. I'm not sure why, but when you feel shitty, you just want to talk about...a lot. To anyone that will listen.

"I can't believe it was all a sham. I thought she loved me."

Billy humored me.

"She fooled all of us," he said, a little distracted.

Yeah, my head was not in the game.

"Man, seven years. All on one girl," I said as I turned to Billy. "One fucking girl."

"Well," he replied lowly, "you have to admit, you haven't actually been beating them off with a stick my friend."

I jerked my head toward him and glared.

Startled by the abrupt and honest comment from Billy, I heard the ref blow the whistle and as I turned back to react, I remember seeing a white and black checkered sphere spinning toward me as blackness flashed.

Yes. Right in the forehead between my eyes.

It all happened in slow motion when I thought about it later. I remember being able to read the *Adidas* label on the ball right before it struck my head.

Billy told me I was out for over a minute.

The light faded in and I opened my eyes. I woke up to Billy's out-of-focus mug standing over me. He was smiling like he just got laid.

"Bright side—you saved a goal," he said.

Like I'm concerned about the score—we were getting our asses kicked. I sat up, moaned, wiped the drool/snot from my mouth and felt that red spot on my forehead. When I stood in the mirror later I could read **sabiba**.

"Bad news—I think you gotta concussion dude."

Billy helped me up and I don't remember walking off the field. I was thinking that it was going to be a late night talking to Billy because I knew that asshole wouldn't let me sleep if he thought I had a concussion.

I guess everyone clapped when I got up and walked off. Funny thing, the biggest cheer I ever got while playing was when I had to leave the game because of an injury (I didn't score a lot of goals). Billy helped me off with one arm over his shoulder and I made my way.

Now, I don't know why, but it was like the sun was a perfect spotlight on that girl I saw in the stands. She stood up from her seat and began walking down the stairs, all in slow motion of course.

I made it off the field as she was making her way down the stadium steps when our eyes met. She stopped and I felt my heart race. My head was heavy. Something was going to give. Billy lost his grip on me and I hit the ground, knees first. My head followed as it slammed into the track that enveloped the barrier of the field.

I remember what I saw when I was out again, but it was difficult to describe. I was in my apartment, it was dark, and there were a lot of people. I couldn't hear anything, but everyone looked like they were having a good time mingling, and some were jumping and dancing to the music I couldn't hear. I was floating through the crowd, not flying above them, just hovering through them. I was drawn to a light that was coming from an open door. Everyone else there didn't notice it like I did. I know because I checked. I felt invisible. I walked through the door. I saw the girl I noticed at the stadium as I passed through the doorway and the spotlight hit her at the end of my tunnel vision.

I wanted to find out who she was.

I know that I was "awake" at the game, but everything was fuzzy and I didn't start to remember anything until after I got home. Billy was there to make sure that I was okay. Good guy, but I remember being annoyed because I was tired and wanted to sleep. He wouldn't let me. Like I said, I had an awesome new forehead tattoo. He went and got an ice pack ready and told me to put it over my **sabiba**.

I was inebriated and I just started talking about whatever came to mind. Of course I talked about *her*.

"Did you see her Billy?"

"Who?"

"I'm not sure, some girl."

I felt so tired and wanted to doze off. Billy humored me; allowing me to babble on.

"She was so…so pretty. She…was sweet looking and gentle. I noticed her leaving as I fell. She had her hair up in a ponytail."

"I love the ponytail," he said.

"Me too," I replied. "It's so…so cute. She had this delicate little smile. Her hair bobbed up and down as she descended the steps."

I remember seeing her face in that moment.

"There was this holy glare about her as if she were the only one that stood out among one-hundred people. I wish I would've gotten her number."

"Okay," he said. "You got hit really hard."

I did.

For all the current happenings…

…you can join my email list:

http://eepurl.com/bhD6qb

I generally put out one a month and talk about movies, television, and the status of my writing in general.

About the author…

…Clintington was born and raised in and around Idaho and has lived there the majority of his life. He has been a cook, a dispatcher, a camera man, a video editor, a sandwich maker, a donut fryer, a direct care staff, a developmental specialist, a policy writer, and a social media content editor. If he's not at work, watching football, or writing—he's most likely with his son, at a park or on the beautiful greenbelt. He managed to earn a degree in television broadcast, and like most people, doesn't currently use his degree in his field…He lives in southwest Idaho with his son.

Website: clintington.com
Amazon Author Page: https://authorcentral.amazon.com/gp/profile
Twitter: @clintingtons
Facebook: https://www.facebook.com/clint.harrington.

www.ingramcontent.com/pod-product-compliance
Lightning Source LLC
LaVergne TN
LVHW041247080426
835510LV00009B/618